s   rain

ALSO BY CHANA BLOCH

POETRY

The Secrets of the Tribe
The Past Keeps Changing
Mrs. Dumpty
Blood Honey

TRANSLATION

The Song of Songs (with Ariel Bloch)
Yehuda Amichai, *The Selected Poetry* (with Stephen Mitchell)
Yehuda Amichai, *Open Closed Open* (with Chana Kronfeld)
Dahlia Ravikovitch, *A Dress of Fire*
Dahlia Ravikovitch, *The Window: New and Selected Poems*
    (with Ariel Bloch)
Dahlia Ravikovitch, *Hovering at a Low Altitude: The Collected Poetry*
    (with Chana Kronfeld)

SCHOLARSHIP

Spelling the Word: George Herbert and the Bible

swimming in the rain

NEW AND SELECTED POEMS

1980-2015

Chana Bloch

Autumn House Press

pittsburgh

"Autumn House" and "Autumn House Press" are registered trademarks owned by Autumn House Press, a nonprofit corporation whose mission is the publication and promotion of poetry and other fine literature.

Autumn House Press Staff

Michael Simms: Founder and Editor-in-Chief
Eva Simms: Co-Founder and President
Giuliana Certo: Managing Editor
Christine Stroud: Associate Editor
Chris Duerr: Assistant Editor
Sharon Dilworth, John Fried: Fiction Editors
J.J. Bosley, CPA: Treasurer
Anne Burnham: Fundraising Consultant
Michael Wurster: Community Outreach Consultant
Jan Beatty: Media Consultant
Heather Cazad: Contest Consultant
Michael Milberger: Tech Crew Chief

Autumn House Press receives state arts funding support through a grant from the Pennsylvania Council on the Arts, a state agency funded by the Commonwealth of Pennsylvania, and the National Endowment for the Arts, a federal agency.

ISBN: 978-1-938769-00-9
Library of Congress Control Number: 2014945510

FOR DAVE

CONTENTS

From *The Secrets of the Tribe* (1980)

From *The Past Keeps Changing* (1992)

From *Mrs. Dumpty* (1998)

From *Blood Honey* (2009)

★

swimming in the rain

NEW POEMS, 2010-2015

SWIMMING IN THE RAIN

Swaddled and sleeved in water,
I dive to the rocky bottom and rise
as the first drops of sky

find the ocean. The waters above
meet the waters below,
the sweet and the salt,

and I'm swimming back to the beginning.
The forecasts were wrong.
Half the sky is dark

but it keeps changing. Half the stories
I used to believe are false. Thank God
I've got the good sense at last

not to come in out of the rain.
The waves open
to take in the rain, and sunlight

falls from the clouds
onto the face of the deep as it did
on the first day

before the dividing began.

A MARRIAGE

Theirs was the one with the noisy bedsprings.
How does a child solve a riddle like that?
Scritchity-screech
—are they fighting again?

Theirs was a marriage of drums and cymbals,
a clashing-and-carping, nagging-and-clamoring
performed day in, day out.

Your mother wanted me dead or alive.
His story of the year they met, retold
in the cancer ward. He was teasing her.
She was laughing too! And I looked away
as if I'd caught them in the act.

Out in the corridor she outdid his story:
"Daddy wanted to make love.
I told him, But honey, your back!
You know what your father answered?
There's nothing wrong with my front."

I watched her shave him in the hospital bed.
She was so tender it left me confused
—one hand cupped to his chin, the other
stroking his cheek with the razor.

CLEOPATRA'S NOSE

Le nez de Cléopatre, s'il eut été plus court,
toute la face de ta terre aurait changé.
— Pascal, *Pensées*

If my nose had been shorter, my whole life
would have turned out different.
Mine was a June egg, that much I know,
but which of the two hundred million spermatozoa
whipped its ambitious tail faster, faster,
and made it to the ovum first?
One more kiss in that noisy bed, one more
creak of the springs and I could have been
somebody else: blue eyes, red hair. If my father
hadn't come to this country when there was
still time, I'd be speaking Russian
or sunk in the ditch at Babi Yar.
If my mother hadn't stepped out on the porch
where he could quietly
give her the eye. If I
had met you, love, when we were young,
this nose of mine
notwithstanding. If I could decipher
that dream of yours and know
how many years we have left,
fat years or lean—
                    If your grandma had balls,
my father would shrug in his Russian Yiddish,
she'd be your grandpa.

BEAUX ARTS

They knew something about pleasure, too,
those painters—how well they understood
it may be compounded
of the simplest elements, the merest trace
of water or light.

Courbet's *L'Origine du monde*, for instance.
The bedclothes are thrust aside
and a woman's fleshy thighs
sprawl across the canvas toward you
as you approach.

Courbet studies his nude with the diligence
of a lover. And lets you see
in the reddish fur
at the body's threshold
a hint of wet

like the dab of white in the iris
that lights the eye.

THE HALL OF HUMAN ORIGINS

American Museum of Natural History

Two sets of footprints in the squelch
of damp volcanic ash,
the only trace of a hominid couple
crossing the African plain
three million years ago.

It must have been raining.
The world is bare
except for a few scattered trees
painted on the sky,
and those two, out in the open,
making their way to us.

Male and female created he them
of wire and plaster,
clothed in the coarse body hair
we keep at armpit and groin,
the two of them walking
upright like us.

His hand on her shoulder,
his arm holding her close
—that human gesture we like to think
we thought up.

HAPPINESS RESEARCH

Rain over Berkeley! The birds are all out
delivering the news.
The evening is wet and happy tonight.
"Is there more to happiness than feeling happy?"
the moral philosophers inquire.

Research has shown
if you spot a dime on the sidewalk
you're more likely to tell the professor your life
is fine, thank you. The effect
generally lasts about twenty minutes.

Scientists are closing in on
the crowded quarter of the brain
where happiness lives. They like to think
it's hunkered down
in the left prefrontal cortex.

"Even in the slums of Calcutta
people on the street describe themselves
as reasonably happy." Why not be
reasonable? Why not in Berkeley? Why not
right now, sweetheart, while the rain
is stroking the roof?

The split-leaf philodendron is happy
to be watered and fed.
The dress I unbuttoned is more than glad
to be draped on the chair.

THE ARK

It's biblical, the papers are saying.
Let it rain! We'll ride it out together,
the two of us—

but what's that scrabbling up in the rafters?

Something is gnawing a hole
with its clever incisors,
inching its whiskers along the walls,
sniffing its way to the tufted
shelter of the attic.
Insulation we installed
to keep out the wind.

"They come in pairs," says Pest Control
with a brisk show of teeth.
"Did you think they were
napping up there?"
He sets the traps, a raisin for each,
and baits us: "Who owns this place?"

All night under the covers
we can hear them in the crawl space
stealing the softness between the joists,
building a nest for their little ones.

TRY, TRY AGAIN

A sullen aunt at the scandal
of other women's babies,
I lived with the latest edition
of *Infertility*,
the calendar's cross-stitch
of little red *Xs*,
the doctor's breezy "Try again."
Each month there was blood,
a punctual failure.
Be fruitful and multiply!
Lashing myself to the effort,
I nearly undid the three of us:
me in my black chemise,
white-knuckled, glum,
the father-to-be in my bed
almost incidental,
the child-to-be glittering away
in its lunar orbit.

CONDUIT

for Benjamin and Jonathan

1

My father stirring sugar in a glass of tea
and I at his bedside, asking
little questions that fit inside
the big ones I didn't dare ask.
He might have figured out he was dying.

2

I'm dying. Not to worry: not any time soon,
I hope. But just so you know.

I keep asking myself,
Should I burn my journals?

3

Such a quiet man, my father.
As a child I learned to read
the blanks between the words.
More blanks than words.

What was he taking with him
into his death?
I sat there day after day translating
his unquiet eyes.

4

What a narrow conduit
between parent and child,
cramped as a mail slot.

It's a wonder anything gets through.

5

My father woke from agitated sleep.
Cossacks pounding on the door.
In the terrified silence of the hospital room,
I heard him crying for his mother.

6

I saved a picture Jonathan made at six:
black hair bristling, the face bright green,
legs planted apart like stanchions,
the belly a fiery furnace.
"That's what you look like when you're angry."

He was right about that fire.
I burned a lot of things in secret.

7

I wanted to save the two of you
from the deadness that lived in our house.
Even smoke-blind, I could always see you.
It was you who saved me.

Would it help you to know
the scope of my confusions?

Night after night, I recorded
the unabridged version of the day,
black ink on blue-lined paper,
then hid it away.

The key to the safe is under the sugar bowl.

DIVORCE

I choked him in a dream and woke up
choking.

My anger frightened me.
"Sharpen your anger," the psychic said.
"You will need that anger if you want
to leave him."

He was still cleaving to me.
A man shall cleave unto his wife.
The knives in my kitchen drawer
wouldn't cut butter.

Once there were silky
tethers to bind us. How to forget?

I needed a blade so sharp
it could slash
whatever still lived between us.
That's what she told me:
a nice clean cut.

Her hand cleaved the air and it shuddered—

half that silk was mine.

HESTER STREET, 1898

No one told them to smile
and they're too busy anyway
with their wooden pushcarts:
Aprons! Prayerbooks! Pickles in brine!
They regard the camera with suspicion.
Butting, shoving, elbow and shoulder,
they tilt the street off-frame.

This is the world they dreamt of
when they slept in mud and misery?
If you climb the skyscrapers up to the sky
you can feel the moon on your cheek,
cool and shivery, like calf's-foot jelly.

Yesterday's laundry waves from the fire escape,
catching a bit of breeze;
a barbershop pole unwinds
its carnival stripes. *Life is better already!*
Better and better.

This they believed, this they taught diligently
unto their children,
who taught it to me.

Whatever I give you, my sons,
I can't give you that.

SUMMER IN THE CITY, 1947

after Helen Levitt

Your mudder is a Hore
chalked on the sidewalk
where the little girls
wiggle their shoulders,
flutter their skirts
in sluggish August heat.
On the stoop, their keepers
are fanning themselves.

"Just the reverse," her Leica says.
"The papas are glued to the stoop
by the sweat of their pants,
the mamas slump,
August is a bummer,
but look at those girls!
Their ankle socks,
their jivey feet."

THE INNOCENTS

I warned my son about strangers
and candy, as a mother should,
but at four he was baffled:
"I didn't know grown-ups be bad."

At his wedding I lifted a glass
and prayed like a mother
for all the naked unknowing
under his three-piece suit.

And his bride in a satin
like moon on snow.

Listen, God:
You might have thought twice
before talking tough to Eve
—a motherless child,
and what's more, a new bride.

I mean, to be innocent is to fall
for snake talk, a language
it takes skill and damage to learn.

LATE SELF-PORTRAIT

after Rembrandt

The mirror is quick to assess him;
he declines to humor it with a smile.
His hundredth report on the loss of illusions.
Lines scored in his brow.

Forget the young man preening
in velvet and bravado,
his elbow planted on stone.
Now it's the mahlstick that steadies his hand.

The master at work in his painter's cap
—the self in that portrait
has the heft of impasto, a life
laid on year after year.

Canny eyes, clown nose, the mouth
defiant: *I've seen what passes
for beauty in the world.
Let someone else pay tribute.*

JULY IN THE BRONX, 1971

Two boys are setting off firecrackers
on the spitting-hot city sidewalk.
I shout out the window: "Stop! Stop it!"
Their answer is another burst.

"For God's sake, my father's *dying*."
They shrug, run away.
Slink back.

Gray pajamas, sweaty, his face a soft white
flag of surrender.
"I wanted to live a little,"
in a raspy voice. Past tense.

"If my old man caught me smoking
when I was a boy,
he'd beat me to ribbons."
The look on his face retrieves
the smoking, not the beating.

Outside on the sidewalk nothing is forbidden.
A puff of cloud rises and rides the air,
sweet whiff of liberty,
acrid, alluring.

IN EXTREMIS

I owe a cock to Aesclepius, Crito,
said Socrates
(the women dismissed, the companions
forbidden to weep)
as the cold ascended from footsole to head.
See that it's paid.

The words of the dying are subject
to the law of scarcity.

I stood at the bedside, weeping, prepared
to wait. Soon enough
I'd be rubbing two words together
for a bit of heat.

I was salvaging every spark
in a notebook with a marbled cover,
getting it all down. The words of the dying
are a last bequest
and I was his firstborn.

My father on morphine had a new
theory of communication.
The remote control, he began,
I'll tell you tomorrow.
And then he died.

WHITE HEAT

Last Friday a man was struck by lightning.
"My friends heard it strike,
saw smoke rising from my body.
My shoes flew off!"
In the front page photo he looks abashed.

My grandma was afraid of lightning.
*If you feel a storm coming, cover your head
and pray.* Her house in the old country
had a prayerworthy
roof of thatch.

Heat gathers drop by drop till the cloud
cannot contain it. Lightning
sizzles across in a burst of ozone,
the darkness blanches,
a live bolt crazes the lid of sky.

I live in a house that's bolted to bedrock,
certified weatherproof,
with double-pane windows,
front door of solid oak.

I'm afraid of safety.
When the lights go out, I'm at the window,
watching a live wire ignite
that fire of water and air.
I want to see what can kill me.

MUIR WOODS

for Dave

I slipped into the hollow
blackened trunk of a redwood
one foggy Sunday
and crooked my finger.

"A forest nymph!" you laughed.
In a wink you're inside.
What a fine and private place to kiss
in the wit of the moment.

Inside this house of ours,
charred walls we can touch
at the core of the living tree.

The scars left by lightning fires
are sleek and cool to our hands.
We are the only heat.

MORNING GLORY, 1999

After supper, the old ladies stay at the table.
"Tell us something special that happened today?"
"I ate a baked potato."
"My daughter called me."
Each one has a bed and dresser in her room,
a flowered towel on a hook.

She gets dressed for dinner when I visit.
A dab of lipstick, a hankie in her pocket.
And earrings! I watch her threading them
into her lobes. She can still do that.
She was a pretty woman, my mother.

"Bring me a glass of water, not too cold.
The doctor gives me such little pills.
It's not getting better."

"It's not getting better," she repeats, a little louder,
in case I missed her meaning.
Then close your eyes, Mama, and make a wish.
She gives me a sharp look
and checks to see what's left of the day.

And if she hasn't died, she's still alive
in that fairy tale with the others,
long after dark,
lifting the fretted silk of her face
toward the table lamp.

AUNT GRETA'S LAST WORDS

It was the youngest son who found her
curled up like a child in her flowered nightie
on the floor near her bed:
body, blunt pencil, cane, rictus,
the final version
of her practiced smile.

That smile was her instrument,
whetted and ready.
Meine kinder, may you always be
as happy as Papa and I.

She of the moiré dress, service for twelve
just so on the table:
forks on the left, knife on the right,
cutting edge under the plate.
So wird's gemacht.

Just a few breaths left
when she scrawls on a slip of paper
Rudy gets the Dürer.

Rudy!

Her will be done:
dressed in her blue wool suit
as she ordained
and laid out in style
for a long eventful afterlife.

NURSING A GRUDGE

You made it, so it's yours
to cradle, swaddle.

How it clamors for you
till it latches on.

So naked a thing,
you can't help giving in.

No one sees you like this—
aroused, seduced.

No one mentions
the pleasure.

When you feed it, it grows.
What darling teeth it has!

And when it bites, the pain
is yours too,

the stab of tenderness
swelling your breast.

Don't give it up, oh no,
not yet.

FORTRESS

Silence is a strenuous language
but we have chosen it.
A shut door, a shrug,
stone upon stone.

The stones have a history.
They were pulled from the rubble
of an earlier weekend
when words were still in use.

After each skirmish we retreat
to warm ourselves at a silence.
And still it's cold.
Let the cold be our comfort!

This is the house that rancor built.
We live in fear.
                A single word
could topple the walls.

CHIAROSCURO

Before the light was divided from darkness,
what was it like, that chaos?
A brilliant shadow? An absence
lit from within?
This is not a question. I'm tired of living
in the land of answers.

At school I'd wave my flag of five fingers,
pleased to produce
just what the teacher ordered.
I needed to get it right.

I knew a man whose first love
was numbers, how sane they are.
Feelings! he blurted, startling himself and me.
Sometimes I wish I didn't have them.

My feelings know more than I do,
and what do they know?
He left me laughing and crying at the same time.

And what did he know without his feelings?
Four currencies, three fine wines,
two fountain pens, one blue, one black,
the capital of every poor country in the world.

THE SEDUCTIONS OF THE GOLDEN MOON

In bed with him for the last time, I was busy
previewing memories.
The way he said, "Let's go upstairs, *hmm?*"
The way his whiskey drawl
quickened when he said it.

Or the winter solstice
when the moon was beaten gold,
gorgeous as Agamemnon's death mask.
It was larger than usual, he told me,
closer to the earth.

The beginning was easy: following the star chart
in the palm of the hand. He traced
my life line to the blue in my wrist,
the shiver in my arm.

Almost at once the middle got underway,
prickly intimations of The End,
which, as it happened, happened
more than once.

We need distance to see a dead thing whole.
Now it's scrubbed clean
as a plot summary. The messy elements
were mopped up by the universe.

THE MEMORY ARTIST

The memory artist has a brutal aesthetic:
delete, delete.
Obsessed with endings, she's known to cut out
the beating heart of what happens.

She understands everything backwards.
That's why she foreshortens the past,
gives it an elegant taper
that looks like Fate.

"We were so happy at first" is allowed
a single line
in the authorized version.

And what about the beginning, the startled kiss
when the paint of day was still wet,
the moment still opening?

She's an artist, you understand—gifted
but troubled. Don't trust her,
not for an instant,
not with your life.

THE REVISED VERSION

1:1   God hovered over the welter and waste
on the face of the deep.

1:2   His brooding condensed
in droplets of light
and conceived the shore of speech.

1:3   And he cried, *Yehí! Let-it-be!*

1:4   From his own breath he fashioned
that command
and he called it *good.*

1:5   He called everything *good*
in the beginning.

1:6   Night fell, the first of many.

THE LITTLE ICE AGE

Europe shivered for centuries in the Little Ice Age.
Rivers froze; crops failed;
people chewed on pine bark,
implored the stubborn heavens:
Lord, have mercy!

That's why the Stradivarius cries so convincingly.
It's the wood remembering,
the stunned wood shuddering,
too numb to grow,
the tree rings huddled close against the cold.

IN HIS MERCY

Now he knows you are hungry
noblesse obliges him to be kind.
If you let him, he'll find a way to give
and take with the same hand.

Much is promised, that much is certain.
Whatever he is ready to grant
he may regret once he divines
it's something you really want.

I'm happy to help, he insists,
and puts out his cigarette
in a pat of butter. Then, in his mercy,
he smiles. And that's that.

The smile is happy with itself
but the butter's a mess. How it longs
not to go soft! to keep its edge!
Oh but the hot ash stings.

TINNITUS

When the astronomers point their ears
at the silence between the stars,
what they hear is a hissing sound, a residual wind
from the eruption of time.

I get it lately without antennas.
My canine brain
picks up frequencies few people register
—the static of the spheres,
the very air taking a breath.

The ancient Egyptians
poured tree sap and frankincense into their ears.
The Romans tried cucumber juice.

Some days the din in my head gets so bad
nothing will stop it but the blast
of people breaking
on the hour, the news of the world.

DEATH MARCH, 1945

for Ben-Zion Gold

"There was a muddy ditch at the side of the road
where the road took a sudden turn. If I could jump—."
Five *Muselmänner* abreast, the trekking dead,
skeletons on the march to some other camp.

"I came up with a plan: if it wasn't already too late,
if the weather held, if the guard didn't turn his head,
by the grace of dark I'd make my way to the right
and take my chances. Chances were all I had."

"Where in that hell did you find the nerve to live?
You knew what lay ahead if you were caught."
I thought he'd say, "No choice. Jump or be killed,"

but he wasn't giving lessons on being brave.
"I was loved," he said, "when I was a child."
I tell his story every chance I get.

- The sign on the wooden bunk reads DO NOT TOUCH. When no one was looking, I touched.

- The war lived in a radio in the kitchen and my father listened.

- "They would've made a nice cake of soap out of me," said the fat man. And laughed.

- The American students wanted to bear the pain of the dead, so they had numbers tattooed on their skin, indelible blue-on-white.

- In the last war, some Israeli soldiers wrote serial numbers on the arms of their Palestinian prisoners. "It wasn't tattoos," they explained. "Just ink."

- "The Germans will never forgive the Jews for Auschwitz," observed the Israeli psychiatrist.

THE OLD TORMENTS

We leave them on the other side of the river.
We are taught to leave them.
Let them be left
till the weather eats them.

When we come this way again
we will find them, bones and shards.
Some bearing teeth marks. Some
broken or charred.

Because time is anesthetic,
we study the bones without emotion.
If we wait long enough, we come as tourists
to the disaster museum.

Borrowed pain.

But let a new torment put forth
a hand and touch you—*skin*
for skin—touch your very flesh,
your bone—

INSIDE OUT

It is either serious or it isn't.
The indeterminate mass, 14.8 cm long,
is either a cyst or a tumor.
If a tumor, either benign or malignant.
If malignant, either slow-growing
or aggressive, in which case
they may contain it. If not,
no one else will recall
this unseasonable day of waiting
exactly as you felt it, from the inside out
—the way the heat of your mind
dropped a few degrees
and grew very quiet. The sediment
settled. You managed to divert
yourself with words. Then
you consulted the uncommon
clarity of the sky. A mild
translucent blue: a sign,
perhaps. The leaves held still
in the almost imperceptible breeze,
though at the tips of the branches
the first buds of spring
were so closefisted
you couldn't be sure
whether you saw them, or not.

DELUGE

Out here, North of Eden, the sky
makes no promises;
one moody cloud and the pressure
plummets. A cold eye keeps watch
even in the rage of heat.

Work is work, but the storms
are historic. Today the sky came unhinged
and the waters lashed
our shoes, our glasses, our helpless clothes.

That immortal weather was a bore.
Too civil. Too many grapes on the vine.
Morning fog, a mild obliging light,
and no rain, not a drop, from May till September.

We might have lulled ourselves
into living forever.

SEPTEMBER SONG

I've got my mother
secured by two magnets to the freezer door.
We're the same age, almost.
A cold day for both of us,
but she's not complaining.

It's a long long while from May
to Wherever, she sings off-key.
Ten years since she died, and she's got
my attention.

See how she managed
Glue Factory Road, all rocks and hard places,
with her walker, her pillbox, her purse
of sorrows, her freckled hands?

She used to put those hands to work
stripping and chopping,
tchik-tchok on the cutting board.
How did she manage
to chop without looking, to speak
without stopping to think?

She made those knuckly fingers of hers
button her beige sweater
inch by inch. Eighty years
to complete the course from
"I can button this all by myself"
to "I can still button."

What a trouper you are! I salute her,
more generous than I used to be.
You never knew me, she comes back quietly,
and lately that's an invitation,
not a complaint.

THE JOINS

Kintsugi *is the Japanese art of mending
precious pottery with gold.*

What's between us
seems flexible as the webbing
between forefinger and thumb.

Seems flexible but isn't;
what's between us
is made of clay

like any cup on the shelf.
It shatters easily. Repair
becomes the task.

We glue the wounded edges
with tentative fingers.
Scar tissue is visible history

and the cup is precious to us
because
we saved it.

In the art of *kintsugi*
a potter repairing a broken cup
would sprinkle the resin

with powdered gold.
Sometimes the joins
are so exquisite

they say the potter
may have broken the cup
just so he could mend it.

AT THE BORDER

for Nina

My hand slips past the guard rail
of the hospital bed,

date of birth on my wristband,
date of death postponed.

By the grace
of a scalpel blade

I have made it across
the border just

in time. My blessing hand rests
on Nina's great naked belly,

Liliana treading water,
headed for land,

her millions of eggs
already alive inside.

the secrets of the tribe

SHEEP MEADOW PRESS, 1980

WATCHING

for my father

You and I used to talk about
Lear and his girls
(I read it in school,

you saw it on the Yiddish stage
where the audience yelled:
Don't believe them,

they're rotten)—
that Jewish father and his
suburban daughters.

Now I'm here with the rest,
smelling the silences,
watching you

disappear.
What will it look like?
Lost on the bed

without shoes, without lungs,
you won't talk
except to the wall: *I'm dying,*

and to the nurse: *Be*
careful, I
may live.

What does a daughter say
to the bones
that won't answer—

Thank you to the nice man?
Daddy?
The last time

we went to the Bronx Zoo,
the elephants were smelly as ever,
all those warm Sundays,

the monkeys as lewd.
But they put the penguins
behind curved glass

with a radiant sky
painted on the far wall.
And all those birds

lined up with their backs to us
watching the wrong
horizon.

BURIAL

The man who makes coffins knows
they could have been ships,
they are built so final.

When the dead set sail in them,
the waves of earth reach up and
collapse
in the old rhythms.
The hiss and spray of the dirt.

I saw a man set adrift once
with only a shroud on him.
The earth rained on me in my sleep.

The coffin swings in its tackle
and sinks down.

When I came back to say goodbye
you were nobody's father
wrapped in a hospital tarp,
tied neck and ankle like cargo.

OUR FATHER

Our father of mud
we built a house of you
made you a roof
In that dark square
we were safe

Our father of straw
we could see you burn
till the sky came through
till the cold
pushed through the broken spaces
Our father of ash

We shovel the darkness over you
carve your name
on a door that won't open
leave these pebbles behind us
at your house

Our father
of stone

IN THE BEGINNING

PARADISE

They were tall as the trees.
The sun spoke in the branches, the hand
reached, the quick
scoop of the hand grew full
when it wanted.

Now the trees close over us, slowly
we carry
everything with us,
carved in our palms.

We keep our heads down like burrowing animals
that can't see in daylight.

BROTHERS

Cain blunders down alleyways of
barren towns, the suburbs
of memory.

No one speaks his language,
no one knows what ghost
he strokes in his dreams.

What do these strangers
see in his face?
    They never felt

God's fingerprint
burn.

★

Squinting, we measured each other,
hungry for the same
mess of love, our
birthright.

We ate fast, watching
for an advantage.

Our smile was made of teeth,
the first
human weapons.

FLOOD

Yawning, the rain still drips
from memory,
damps the small dust down.
Sun buds in the sky.
Trees shake out their quills.
Birds sing, gingerly.
New grass whets its blades.

The great hulk of houseboat beached
on top of Ararat.
The timbers crack as they dry.
It will stay there forever, shrinking
invisibly.

On land our stiff
white bird legs
wobble.

The last waters lap and ebb,
lap and ebb
in the ear's conch.

THE BINDING OF ISAAC

The patriarch in black takes
candle and knife
like cutlery,
rehearsing under his breath
the Benediction
on the Death of an Only Son.

Isaac stoops under the raw wood,
carries his father on his back.

On the woodpile
Isaac waits, girlish,
fever trilling under his skin.

He will remember the blade's
white silence,
a lifetime
under his father's eyes.

THE RECKONING

Green cattle pasture
in the fatlands

of Pharaoh's sleep,
up to their knees in dream.

The brothers, scheming,
the coat striped with blood,
the old man's knees:
this is what comes of dreamers.

Joseph knows,
counting the cows to
Pharaoh's
narrow
face.

*

The brothers are set at the table,
each in his appointed seat.
They have come all this way
to swallow
the past.

The stranger their brother
stands before them
undeciphered.

No one speaks.

No one is what he was.

EXILE

What happened to the ten lost tribes
is no great mystery.
They found work, married, grew smaller,
started to look like the natives
in a landscape nobody chose.
Soon you couldn't have picked them out of a crowd.

And if they'd stayed where they were,
what happiness would they have endured?
We can't believe in it.

The face of the cities scares us,
day and night empty us till
we are no longer
God's chosen.

For a while we camp out under the strange trees,
complaining, planning a return.
But we have taken out papers and become citizens.

THREE STUDIES FOR A HEAD OF JOHN THE BAPTIST

1

His beard spreads in front of him
as if in the bath,
the little hairs crinkled.

It's a copper platter, embossed
with palm trees and turtledoves,
polished to a high gloss.

The head sits off-center.
The chill of metal; oriental spices.

His eyes look around, curious,
as the musicians tune up.

2

At the corner, as the sun cut,
I held my head in my hands.

It was heavy,
like a bag of groceries
I shift from one hip to the other.

I wanted to set it down somewhere,
a windowsill,
a doorway, a low brick step
where it could flash its carved grin all day for the children.

3

The elegance
of the sharpened knife—it's not
the head that imagines it
but the back of the neck
that must carry such a weight
on its bent stalk,

that cannot speak.

YOM KIPPUR

Our new clothes fool no one.
A year of days. The fingernails
keep growing, even
in life.

We are tight for the winter, brooding
in this vat of used air.
As if we could hatch
some glory out of sitting still.

What shrinks inside us, this grit
that rattles in our throats
tells us only
to go on getting older.

But the eyes want, the fingers, the emptiness
of the mouth
wants something to speak to, some lost
horn of a mouth with its unpredictable answers.

On the eastern wall, the lions
stand fast,
raising their braided heads,
their gold tongues whetted.

THE CONVERTS

On the holiest day we fast till sundown.
I watch the sun stand still
as the horizon edges toward it. Four hours to go.

The rabbi's mouth opens and closes and opens.
I think *fish*
and little steaming potatoes,
parsley clinging to them like an ancient script.

Only the converts, six of them in the corner,
in their prayer shawls and feathery beards,
sing every syllable.
What word
are they savoring now?
If they go on loving that way, we'll be here all night.

Why did they follow us here, did they think
we were happier?
Did someone tell them we knew
the lost words
to open God's mouth?

The converts sway in white silk,
their necks bent forward in yearning
like swans,
and I covet
what they think we've got.

FURNITURE

Last night we talked about God
as metaphor, like
the head of the table
the leg of the chair
God of the Universe.

"I haven't got a God to stand on,"
I said. And flinched.
No thunder.

"Shame on you!
God will punish you," my mother would say,
"if you write on Shabbos."
When I wrote, I pulled down the shade.

In those days there was thunder like furniture moved in heaven.
God came down from the mountain.
My heart ticked evenly as a clock at the head of the bed.
On Friday the candles stood lit on the table,
and four chairs, one at each side,
squaring the round world.

There were crumbs on the tablecloth
and hot wax dripped from the candles
so quietly
we never heard them
go out.

THE LESSON

When she played
those veins
flickered and jumped.

That's what I saw
from the piano bench
under the tasseled lamp

and in the backroom that scarecrow
her mother, dirty rouge
on the cheekbones, the hooded eyes
staring.

Each Tuesday I'd come back,
tugging at my music:
Will I have veins like that
when I learn to play?

The ugliness of the adult world,
how we craved it—
not knowing but wanting.

What a man
does to a lady—whatever
we dreamt of that mystery,

the brutal music
of a real life, yes,
that's what it's like,

whatever could make her blood
stand up like that.

HAPPINESS

"What kind of bird is that twittering now?"
I ask through the window,
all big-city innocence,
and you tell me:
a frog.

As for these birds tugging rubber
worms from the lawn,
or that tree, that immense rooted
broccoli—
let's put the trees back
in marriage.

The day you seduced
a field of cows in your best
bull's voice.
One by one they ambled up,
swaying their comfortable udders.

If this is the world,
we are the only ones in it,
naming the animals, finding
a language. Look
how it comes out,
the ripe apricot of the sun,
like a child's crayoned God.

I am hanging wash on the line.
Our sleeves
wrap me in love.

Like Adam in his first
happiness,
you come out
and pee in the garden.

MAGNIFICAT

I will carry my belly to the mountain!
I will bare it to the moon, let the wolves howl,
I will wear it forever.
I will hold it up every morning
in my ten fingers,
crowing
to wake the world.

This flutter that comes with me everywhere:
is it my fear
or is it your jointed fingers,
is it your feet?

You are growing yourself
out   of   nothing:
there's nothing
at last I can
do: I stop
doing: you
are.

Miles off in the dark,
my dark,
you head for dry land,
naked, safe in salt waters.

Tides lap you.
Your breathing
makes me an ark.

MILK

1

The baby is hollering
libel
           You never come
Why doesn't anyone
ever come

He forgets
last time and the time before
I keep coming
but that's a piece of good news
he can't hold on to

like the nipple that dissolves
when his sucking stops

How he gropes for it, hunger
pumping the valves of his mouth
the fierce
concentration of the fists

Even in his sleep he's trying
to suck comfort
from the thin air

2

Two eyes and the fur of the brows
the minimum

requirements for a face
he gathers in his clear eyes
that have tested nothing but darkness

The breast finds him
like his own
wet fist

His mouth thinks
we are one flesh

He doesn't know we are outside
each other
I am dark years away
he will live all his life in the world
between us

INFANT

Curled in sleep he contains himself
as a cloth folded over and over withholds
the final truth of its colors.

Soon he will not need me to unfold him.
Every morning he'll hoist his head up
the skinny pole of his body,
take himself down at night.

The bones are already stretching in his sleep.
Pliant as licorice, they'll harden into
the skeleton he dies with.

In his bald face
I can see my father looking back.
The bones of the dead light up his transparent flesh
as in an X-ray
of everything that will become of us.

EATING BABIES

1

Fat
is the soul of this flesh.
Eat with your hands, slow, you will understand
breasts, why everyone
adores them—Rubens' great custard nudes—why
we can't help sleeping with
pillows.

The old woman in the park pointed,
Is it yours?
Her gold eye-teeth gleamed.

I bend down, taste the fluted
nipples, the elbows, the pads
of the feet. Nibble earlobes, dip
my tongue in the salt fold
of shoulder and throat.

Even now he is changing,
as if I were
licking him thin.

2

He squeezes his eyes tight
to hide
and *blink!* he's still here.
It's always a surprise.

Safety-fat,
angel-fat,

steal it in mouthfuls,
store it away
where you save

the face that you touched
for the last time
over and over,
your eyes closed

so it wouldn't go away.

3

Watch him sleeping. Touch
the pulse where
the bones haven't locked
in his damp hair
—the navel of dreams.
His eyes open for a moment, underwater.

His arms drift in the dark
as your breath
washes over him.

Bite one cheek. Again.
It's your own
life you lean over, greedy,
going back for more.

DEER IN THE BUSH

They come down
in the mornings, sniff
the green edges of our lives,
taste the hydrangeas.

Shadows let them.
Their legs springy as twigs,
they step
in a pool of shade,

nosing our flowers,
nudging us out on the porch
to watch them
watch us for a sign.

They study our moving toward them
and won't be fooled,
letting their pleasure wilt on the bush
till they can be sure of us. Wait:

I can see a buck
up on his hind legs, wrestling a
branch down, his velvet mouth
dripping berries.

He's at home in our seasons
like an old uncle
who comes when he pleases and keeps
the secrets of the tribe.

the past keeps changing

SHEEP MEADOW PRESS, 1992

THE FAMILY

Inside the Russian woman there's
a carved doll,
red and yellow to match her,
with its own child inside.
The smallest, light as a salt shaker,
holds nothing
but a finger's breadth of emptiness.

Every morning we are lifted
out of each other,
arms stiff at our sides.
In the shock of daylight
we see our own
varnished faces everywhere.

At night we drop back
into each other's darkness.
A tight round sky
closes over us
like a candle snuffer.

We sleep
staring at the inside.

THE VALLEY OF THE DEAD

1

No one feeds the dead anymore.
No one leaves them juniper berries and melon seeds
in an alabaster bowl.
They have stopped hunting in the ochre marshes.

They used to live forever
on painted wheat.
The sky was flat; the sun skimmed across it
in a boat. At that latitude

there is no twilight. The gods
with their beaked hunger—
falcon, jackal, hawk—
wait, enormous, on the walls.

2

In the long leisure
of heaven

there is no friction, the hand
goes on waving the fan of ostrich feathers,

the ivory bird is called back
as witness

and the chairs with their stiff
clawed feet. Nothing

happens only once.
We perform the past over and over

until we get it right.

3

Whatever you gave me, I used it up right away
for breathing.
That's why nothing is left but amulets,
red paint flaking off the potsherds,
Isis holding out her naked breasts
in both hands—

your hands. Sun edges in
the broken shutter.
                              The rest
turned into body and bread.

The pain is historical, silted under
other sediments,
and it doesn't hurt.

Whatever you gave me, I made it serve,
I couldn't save it
for later. That's why only your handprints
are left, faintly visible,
pressed into the clay.

PRIMER

1

On the kitchen table, under
a dusting of flour, my mother's hands
pressed pastry into the fluted shell
with experienced thumbs.

Mustard-plaster, mercurochrome wand,
blue satin binding of the blanket
I stroked to sleep,
soft tar roof where the laundry
bellied and bleached,
sky veined with summer lightning:

If we were so happy,
why weren't we happy?

2

Dreams sink a deep shaft down
to that first shoe,
bronzed, immortal.

We looked up at a sky of
monumental nostrils, grim tilted
backlit faces.

We learned to shape the letters,
l's and *t*'s looped and tied, small *i*'s
fastened by a dot.

When we stood up, our feet reached the ground.

We wiped the kisses from our cheeks with the back of our hands.

3

I thought I was a grasshopper
in the eyes of giants.
My father set his hand on the doorknob,
slowly, without looking at me;
my mother lifted her hand, the fingertips
Hot Coral.
I thought she was saying *Come here.*

That's why I kept calling them back,
Look, look who I've become!
But it was too late;
he had his jacket on, and she
was smiling at her mouth in the hall mirror.

Now I am huge. This is my
bunch of keys, my silence, my own
steep face. These
are my children, cutting on the dotted lines:
blunt scissors
and a terrible patience.

CHEZ PIERRE, 1961

The skirt's all wrong and the shoes
pinch: thin straps
and little pointed heels. Borrowed clothing.
She crosses her legs under the table.
Uncrosses them.

Heat rises heavy, a raincloud
gathering moisture.
His hand comes down over hers.
Look at those couples—their lives
are already a downpour.

She can't imagine me yet
though she's starting that puzzled
tuck around the mouth,
the one I'm just getting used to.
He draws little *Os* on her palm

with a fingernail, laughing, taking
his time. I still
carry her with me, unfinished,
into the hazard
of other people's hands,

I live with her choices.
The waiter says, *Sweet
or dry?* and wipes the dew from a bottle.
She's got to decide, tonight!
for my life to begin.

GOODBYE

The repairman turns to leave.
A brisk goodbye
slips him out of my story.
Click. He's gone.

Lately I am so hard
people keep sliding off me.

This emptiness sharpens me.
Light prints itself on the plate of memory,
acid burned into metal.

It's thirty years since you and I invented
a ritual for parting.
Back-to-back in the crowded city street,
we walked five paces apart and were swallowed up
by our lives.

When they said *If you eat this fruit
you will die,*
they didn't mean right away.

THE PAST WE STARTED

1

The man at the corner looks like my
dead father. That tightness
around the eyes. He steps off the curb and
I almost stop him
—a stranger, waiting to cross a street
in his own life.

I make him speak
without his knowing it.

2

And you: what I take is not
what you give me, either.
I stall at the window, drawing
a face in steam. *Why did you tell me?*
Don't go. You, quick on the thread of
wherever you're going. Silent,
you close your eyes

the way my father used to. God
of the supper table, hoarding
his words. And I, at the iron
edge of my chair. Any child knows
how to make a feast
of crumbs and silence.

3

The past we started hasn't
finished with us. It chooses a body,
a bait, a jacket
wet in the rain. O my tower
of newspaper, pillar of
smoke—
                    How the light flashed
from his rimless glasses! I am still trying
to make him look up.

CROSSING THE TABLE

I want the language of lovers
before they touch,
when their eyes telegraph
verbs only, because
each word costs.

The way they startle and
contract. *Have they given away*
too much too soon?

Across the table
you're a foreign city
where the natives always talk fast.

A whole life to tell and no time
to tease the words out, crazy
to connect, we
strain like children breaking

into speech.
                You look up: I
step out in frantic English
into the traffic.

WHITE PETTICOATS

If the egg had one drop of blood in it
the rabbis said, "Throw it away!"
As if they could legislate
perfection. Dress the bride
in white petticoats! Let there be

no spot
on your ceremony!
As if we could keep our lives
from spilling
on our new clothes.

That night we came home
strangers, too tired to speak,
fog in the high trees
and a trunk full of shiny boxes
we didn't unwrap.

There's a bravery in being naked.
We left our clothes
on the doorknob, the floor, the bed,
and a rising moon opened its arms
around the dark.

HUNGER

What goes out into the world in boots
comes back
banging a spoon on the scarred table: *More.*

Day comes back dusk, was it
brightness you wanted?

You go out full. Night
brings you home again, dragging
a sack of emptiness.

This is the house that was carved for you
from a single beam of cedar.
Here is your daily manna
washed in dew,
delivered fresh to your dining table.

You've had your seven wishes
and never been grateful.
When all this
vanishes

you'll be back
in that hovel by the sea,
sweeping the bare stones.

NIGHT SHIFT

All night, in the cramp of sleep,
we grind the day-stone between our molars,

we spin
straw into flesh.

It is a form of penance. Locked
in our bodies,

our legs unstrung.
The bed is crowded: you

in your striped pajamas,
me, pillow feathers

with their memories of flight.
Your dreams and mine rise to the ceiling and

hang there, looking down at us
till we beg *Come back,*

come back inside us,
it's almost morning.

FIREWOOD

When you sawed a branch from the pine tree
the white sky submerged us,
a clear fluid brisk as vinegar, and I kept
missing it, kept going out to look at
what I knew wasn't there.

Put it back! I begged, but the branch
was already a pile of logs
stacked and ready for use.
One evening's wood.

The luxury of that low branch hanging down!
We had to duck every time to get past,
it choked out the sun,
nothing but pine needles grew under it.

In the fire I see our faces
losing their shape.
There's no way to change
without touching
the space at the center of everything.

INSIDE

"Is it blue
inside a bluebird?" the child asked.

Then he told me: "A baby's head is all stuffed
with hair. It keeps growing out, frizzy,
till it gets used up. That's why
old men are bald."

THE STUTTER

1

We speak too fast.
The child sits at our table, waiting
his turn. The clock
points a sharp finger. The daily
soup steams,

too hot to eat. Between
words the child thrashes *I-I-I*—
Our patience

takes a deep breath.

2

That high voice—all clumsy fingers—
can't untie
the shoelace fast enough. The master of the house
is counting. The hurt
voice circles
over and over, blunt needle picking at an old
blocked groove.

3

Years ago in a high chair
he drummed wet fists, his face
a knot, *Give me*

words. The fury
beat in his throat. Mother and father, we put
words in his mouth, we

speak harder, faster, we give him
a life to chew on.

AGAINST GRAVITY

1

November. A forty-watt twilight.
You bring me the white of your face
like a letter with an old address,
so rubbed out I can't
decipher it.

I watch you stare up
at the twisted prongs of the fig tree.

You're secreting a silence around you,
iridescent, slippery. I don't know
where the body stops and the outer
darkness begins.

Remember last spring? It was you
who showed me,
pointing up, laughing:
caterpillars held by invisible
threads in the branches,
doing their little dance against gravity.

2

I carried the child for weeks without telling,
letting the secret
feed me. Only you and I knew
and we closed

around each other. I grew a path
we could take without needing
to speak. Light passed between us
at midnight, poured

from a cloudy source and kept
pouring.

3

In the hard light, we study
each other's faces
like the deaf.

When we cut down the pine
we read its story
in the plain script of trees: drought years
and flood years. It's all clear

afterward. At the center the dead
heartwood with its
five cracked spokes. Then the pitted bark
that keeps things out.

RISING TO MEET IT

Pain is the salty element.

All that night I lay
tethered to my breathing. To the pain,
the fixed clock-stare of the walls,
the fingers
combing my tangled hair.
"Ride out the waves," the doctor said.

The first time I touched a man,
what startled me more than the pleasure
was knowing what to do.
I turned to him with
a motion so firm it must have been
forming inside me
before I was born.

I was swimming upstream, the body
solid, bucking for breath, slippery,
wet. An ocean
rolled off my shoulders.

Tonight, strapped to the long night, I miss
the simple
pain of childbirth—

                  No, not the pain
but that rising to meet it like a body
reaching out in desire, buoyant, athletic,
sure of its power.

CHANGELING

Through the half-open door I can hear it
in the other room, breathing.
Branches on glass, a cold blade
scraping my backbone.

One eye like a knot of wood, staring,
one eye torn with rain.
I am yours, it says.
You will learn to live with me.

I beg the window: *Be morning.*
This is still my house.

It stirs, turns over, pulls at the dark.
It always wakes with a cry.
How it whimpers when I approach.

I take it to my breast
and let it bite.

BLUE-BLACK

That road leads only
to the bridge, to the
hiss and slap
of water, the muddy
suck of the bottom.
I know the way.

All winter
I pitched through night in a fury of falling,
falling,
wind in my teeth,
my body an old coat with stones
in its pockets.

I found my body on the bridge.
Fingers locked to the cold rail,
counting, as if
the blue-black
slippery ocean were a hope
to hang onto.

I knew that old coat,
the brown shag, the missing
buttons. I watched
my slow fingers
choosing. My knuckles.
My stubborn feet.

ANNIVERSARY

The metal gate has a crow-cry, almost human.

You'll see, said the elders, speaking
in riddles.

Twenty years, in October.
I stroke the rise of your cheek like a talisman:
sun and wind scored in the dusty ground
of our faces.

                    These planted
fenceposts, the scaling, crude joins, corroded
nails. The sawed-off rounds of the woodpile,
seasoned, waiting
to be used. The feathered seedpod
rolling over and over across the road on its white floss.

Your hand on my shoulder, like a question—

Rosin of sunlight slides up and down
a string of spiderweb,
bowing a high note. The eye
can hear it.

MAMA PUDDING

"You have seven gray hairs," says my son,
my firstborn,
and lifts me off the floor.
Pokes an accusing thumb into
Mama Pudding,
fixes a beam of truth and refuses
to gentle it.

At his age, I'd scour
my elbows with half a lemon
to make them white as a lady's.

My mother sagged in her casing.
Her dress was too bright, her eyelids
gleamed like fish-scales.
I tried on her crimson lipstick,
oh mirror, mirror.

My son slams the door, brings the music
to a boil.

"Make a fist," he says. "Come on, punch my
stomach, hard."
And leans down to admire himself
in my eyes.

His body sends up
little coiled signals, dark pulses, a code
he can almost read.

AT THE OPEN GRAVE

The pickaxe hurts. Caked
bedrock,
hard-packed. The pick
goes after rock bottom.

And the gravedigger in his muddy
rubber-soled shoes. Dirt clings
to the rusted metal, clumps of it,
damp from the last rain.
He flicks it off easily.

Your leftover words, I want
to say them; let them be
said. Let the tree fall in that
forest of yours. One of us
will hear it. Well, then. Let it be
half-heard.

You were telling me something.
In this life we bury the dead
alive. What an austere
discipline,
to turn and walk away.

IN THE LAND OF THE BODY

1

A crooked
finger of pain, a hand, a gloved hand
reaches inside me.
Does this hurt? Does this?

I ask it *Where next?* but it doesn't
know yet. And you

reach for me shyly, as if you
didn't know me,
didn't know either
where to touch. *Is this good?*
Is this?

Your fingers stutter a little
as if the pain
hurt them. Is this how the rest
                                begins?
Your mouth, my body staring, and that hand

twisting inside.

2

He shows me my body translated
into swirls of light on a fluorescent screen.

This is the thorax with its curving
fingers of rib, its thick

ring of fat. These
are the soft blind organs, huddled, the lungs
filled with black air.
This is a transverse section
of the spinal column: a white eye,
a dark pupil.

I'm waiting for him to read
my fortune:
values on a scale, relative
shades of gray.

Inside me everything's in color, glossy,
opaque. A lump of pain
in a hidden pocket.
His voice segmented, exact, he
talks to the picture,
takes a crayon, draws
a burst of rays
around the star he's discovered

but hasn't named.

3

The moment the doctor. *Looks like.*
No way to. Scrubbed hands

scooping. *The size of.* At the mercy
of the body. And to carry it

inside for years, sealed,
without even. *But if.* Not to know

your own. *There have been
cases.* Dear God

I don't believe in. But
what would I. *Tuesday.* The sun

leaves its snail trace across.
It's the waiting that—

4

The good children eat what I set before them,
lick the plate clean
and wait

for an answer. Their feet
dangle above the linoleum.
The big one is doodling a whale,

choosing crayons:
Are you going to die? He adds
gray spotted wings.

The little one draws my face on a beanpole
in a garden
of green nails. He gives me

a loopy skirt, shoes
and a few stiff flowers.
When he bends over to color me in,

I see how careful he is
to keep the colors from spilling
over the lines.

5

A sharp wind
pries at the doorjamb, riddles
the wet sash. Was it just
last week?

We sat at the fireplace, the four of us,
reading *Huck Finn*. I did the Duke,
you the Dauphin, the kids
tossed pillows in the air.
We owned that life.

There's a future loose in my body and I
am its servant:
carrying wood, fetching water.

You cup a hand over my stomach
to feel the dark
dividing.
The hand listens hard.

And the children are practicing
pain: one finger, quick!
through the candle flame.

6

We have chosen each other.
The stranger walks slowly toward me,
a white mask over his words.

I left everything to come here.
They took away my watch.

The children
grew smaller, disappeared.

Where are we going. I lie down
under the thirsty mouths
of the soundproof ceiling.

This room has no windows, no
shadows. The air
burns cold
and the cold is absolute.

We start off together on the long journey.
My sack of flesh closes around him.
My belly
swallows his hands.

7

Mine is small and slow-growing,
floats
at an unknown altitude.

When I sleep, the doctors
sway over my bed. They flicker away
and swim up slippery,
tie my feet down,
cut a vista into my belly.

Everyone lives under a cloud, they say.

Mine chafes the horizon, so small
I will cover it with my hand.

8

And then I rose
to the dazzle of light, to the pine trees
plunging and righting themselves in a furious wind.

To have died and come back again
raw, crackling,
and the numbness
stunned.

That clumsy
pushing and wheeling inside my chest, that ferocious
upturn—
I give myself to it. Why else
be in a body?

Something reaches inside me, finds the pocket
that sewed itself shut, turns it
precipitously
out into the air.

DEATHS I COME BACK TO

The lilacs on the roadside are rusting.
They hold up clusters of lost light,
soft brown stars that wrinkle and go dead.

The deaths I keep coming back to
send up a musky smoke, the slow
burn of decay.

On the forest floor, pale vellum leaves;
rain-tempered pine cones, stained with resin;
pine branches drying their brooms, tails, tufts of red;
a half-eaten stump, the corky wood
flaming upward.

Then the creak of a dry branch,
the cawing of deadwood ready to fall.

Dead leaves on the ground, the watery shadows
of the living:
the sift and sway of light.

In the rutted pine tree
rough stubs of branches go after
the light. I climbed
that tree, too, death after death.

I snap off a branch of hemlock
to carry home, stroking the bright wingtips,
moist green, without memory.

DAY-BLIND

One clap of day and the dream
rushes back
where it came from. For a moment
the ground is still moist with it.
Then day settles. You step onto dry land.

Morning picks out the four
corners, coffeepot, shawl of dust
on a cupboard. Stunned
by brightness, that dream
—where did it go?

All day you grope beneath invisible stars.
The day sky soaks them up
like dreams. If you could see
in the light, you'd see what fires
keep spinning, spinning

around you. They're closer
than you think, pulsing
into the blue. You press
your forehead to the window glass.

They must be out there in all that dazzle.

I climb up here only
to feel small again. Blue liquor
of distances: one sip and I start to lose
size, anger, the sticky burrs
of wanting. *If only, what if*—let the wind
carry it away.

Wave after wave of shadow comes over
the mountain, like some great
migration. Up here
everything's painted the four
bare colors: sky, cloud, rock, shadow.

To be the object of so much weather!
I'm the only one left at the end
of the last act. Everyone has died,
or gone off to be married.

Look how that tree
catches the wind, strains like a kite against
its patch of sky. That's
what I come for.
                    An important cloud
is making its way to some other mountain, to the sea,
scattering finches like poppy seeds.

mrs. dumpty

UNIVERSITY OF WISCONSIN PRESS, 1998

MRS. DUMPTY

The last time the doctors gave up
I put the pieces together
and bought him a blue wool jacket, a shirt
and a tie with scribbles of magenta,
brown buckle shoes. I dressed him
and sat him down
with a hankie in his pocket folded into points.
Then a shell knit slowly
over his sad starched heart.

He'd laugh and dangle his long legs and call out,
What a fall that was!
And I'd sing the refrain,
What a fall!

And now he's at my door again, begging
in that leaky voice,
and I start wiping the smear
from his broken face.

HOSANNA

For the way we met between floors on the staircase
(*He's the one,* said Martha),
for the salt of your cheek and the silky
crook of your elbow,
the secondhand mattress with its geography of stains,
for the spirits of Berkeley whose names
I didn't know yet
(*Jasmine,* said Sharon, *azalea, camellia, rhododendron,*
and I scribbled it all down like a student),
for the sticky
imprint of your sweat up and down my body
as we studied each other,
for your honeymoon kisses at dawn
and Dubrovnik still green (*Have a Good Trip with*
ENA Motoring Oil, the billboard blessing
in Serbo-Croatian),
for the thermos that broke when I opened the car door
(*It's good luck,* we warned each other),
the old woman in the park who offered us dark bread and cheese
with a cackle of *Bitte, bitte,*
the one word of Foreign she knew,
for the red fox that startled us, the two trees that rose
from a single charred trunk,
the monks chanting plainsong in the church near Zagreb
that burned down in the war
(*Hosanna,* they sang),
for each loss that sparks another like kisses
we stay up all night for
wherever they lead.

PLEASE HOLD

You used to imitate a camel
eating—nostrils flared, your dogged
hilarious jaw
sawing left and right. It was easy
to love you then.

I'd start coq au vin
on the poky two-burner,
James Beard propped open with a pot.

That time we dialed Pan Am and danced
to their "Please Hold" fox trot, Mulligan's
honey-slow horn (remember?),
the telephone pressed between us. . . .

We'd drowse off at midnight, a muddle
of arms and legs
till your cock-crow under the covers
awakened us both.

And then there was morning. I'd steal
one last-minute dream
and open my eyes to a blur
of Burma Shave
in the bathroom doorway, a fizz of sunrise

you wiped away, then
two-stepped toward me.

ACT ONE

Hedda Gabler is lighting the lamps in a fury.
From the front row center
we see the makeup streaking her neck
little tassels of sweat
that stain her bodice. She says *yes* to Tesman
and it's like spitting.

We are just-married,
feeling lucky. Between the acts
we stop to admire ourselves in the lobby mirror.

But Hedda—how misery
curdles her face!
She opens the letters with a knife
and her husband stands there
shuffling, the obliging child
waiting to be loved.

Yes, she says, fluffing the pillows
on the sofa, *yes dear,* stoking
the fire. And Tesman smiles. A shudder
jolts through her body to
lodge in mine, and

     oh yes, I can feel that
blurt of knowledge
no bride should know.

ANNUNCIATION

The future
passed through me like light
through a prism, foot-traffic
over a bridge: two children, two
freestanding sons.
I thought I was choosing.
Light spilled through the window,
indifferent. I thought you were
choosing me. The mole on
my shoulder your earlobes our
naked teeth in their lust
to outlive us
drove us together. The past flooded me
in its milky rush to become
forever. The past in its
superabundant
waste. The angel spoke
in fire and tongues, imperturbable,
leaving me
spent on the sheets, a dazed
hand on a belly.

HAPPY FAMILIES ARE ALL ALIKE

1

Flash of truck, blaze of
steel bearing down
burn of rubber on asphalt two tons
thundering to a stop. I can smell it,
can see that trucker
stunned, head down in his hands,
St. Christopher swinging in the window

and across the street on Colusa
in front of the school door,
hands face skinny knees, every part of him
sharply visible, outlined
in yellow light—

my son. His high voice
more plaintive than blaming:
You told me to run.

2

Who told him to run? My fault
forever. A family of before
and after. *Why did you why
did I tell him?* But look,

he's going into the classroom.
He's eating the soggy triangles

of his tuna sandwich. Nothing's
happened to us! Nothing

yet. Once upon a time, we'll say
at the family campfire,
we came *that* close.

SELF-PORTRAIT AT 11:30 P.M.

This is the face I serve nightly
with lace bubbles of almond soap,
head down
in the second degree of fatigue.

These are the baby breasts I buried
in my woman's bosom. Sloped shoulders.
Skinny ribcage, a fist still
beating at the bars.

Black bra, taupe stockings, long slithery
half-slip. The scar
running down my belly, ridged, opalescent.
The wild thatch they shaved off
grew back.

This is my belly, spongy, forgiving,
all its pockets picked clean.
It settles down on the stoop, drowsy:
Once I was adored.

And my feet, with their sturdy
badges of callus. All day
in the mill of my shoes
they grind, obedient.
The skin of the instep
soft as chamois.

TIRED SEX

We're trying to strike a match in a matchbook
that has lain all winter under the woodpile:
damp sulphur
on sodden cardboard.
I catch myself yawning. Through the window
I watch that sparrow the cat
keeps batting around.

Like turning the pages of a book the teacher assigned—

You ought to read it.
It's great literature.

SURPRISE PARTY

1

He's holding the garage door opener in his hand.
Each time he clicks,
he alters the constellations.
He tells me this, elated.
It must be a sign.

Even the psychiatrist says it's a good dream,
but by now she's prospecting, like us,
for anything that glitters a little in the water.

2

We own a house: tan stucco, brown trim,
lamps, lamp-tables, a family
of chairs. The live oak in front
keeps us rooted.
The neighbor's cat waits for us to come home,
pads up the nineteen steps and presents
her belly to be rubbed.

And the children, of course,
our witnesses.

3

Tabbouli, black olives, Moroccan carrots,
the salads gleaming in their oils,
two days of shopping, paring and dicing,

polishing the brass. Then the toasts
and the silly candles,
the children sprawled on the floor.

Lift up your heads, O ye gates!
Linda, the world's latest widow, crowned him
Almighty King of Fifty
with a helmet of straw, his scepter
an orange studded with cloves.

He was better by then, I thought,
though he hadn't been sleeping.
I watched from the doorway, happy.

Today, still fresh from the shower,
full of a tense exuberance,
he finds me in the kitchen.
That's when it started, he wants me
to know—with Linda, there, at the party.
I don't know the welt in my throat

is anger. I take
the dishtowels from the cabinet,
fold them in two, in three,
line up their sky-blue stripes
and put them back again.

THE CONSERVATION OF ENERGY

"Why was that door locked? I want
the front door open when I get home,

and the lights on, the minute
you hear me honking." He slams

the door behind him, dashes
the porcelain bowl from the table.

Drips of oil shiver to the floor,
fork and knife, little wings

of frayed lettuce. A few
bleak words bitten off and I snap

at our son, who enters
laughing. And now

the child is pulling the cat's tail
with both hands. The cat

is storing up minus signs like a battery,
sharpening its claws.

HIGH SUMMER

The sky was blue-violet that evening until 10 p.m., so we drove to a lake in the park and rented a rowboat. There was an island in the middle of the lake, overgrown with willows and moss. Our older son took the oars and rowed us toward the island. The little one sat in the prow and announced: "Hey! I'll be the reporter of swan and duck news."

Sometimes a wave of happiness wells up and wipes everything clean. The water cannot contain itself. The old angers soften and sink down to the sludgy bottom. I laughed when that wave came and lifted the boat from the water.

THE COMFORTERS

1

The cat nosed around the hummingbird
but didn't want him. Sweet bird,
his throat feathers go black
then fuchsia when I tip him to the side.
Who else could I show this to but
you? I'm promoting
reasons for living. Today it's The Miracle
of Change—the rain in California, for instance,
that comes every winter to wash
the cobwebs from the leaves.
But you aren't listening.

When you give me that spooky look
I'll try anything.

2

"What are you planning for your
retirement?" sang the neighbor to my father
propped on his final flowered pillow.
She stirred the coffee I brought her,
forked up her cake
and doled out comfort to my father the way

I talk to my husband: slowly,
as if he were a child, and too loud,
as if he were deaf or foreign, and so careful,
profusely careful, choosing
each wrong word.

RELIC

That hanger I stole from the honeymoon hotel—
I've hidden it away. The kings of Europe used to kill
for a relic like that, a crumb
of the true manna, one drop of Mary's milk
in a jewelled vial.

I want you back, whoever
you used to be. I'm saving the way you'd take
the steps to our front door two at a time,
singing *Anyone home?* as your key turned
its trick in the lock.

TWENTY-FOURTH ANNIVERSARY

I hung my wedding dress
in the attic. I had a woolen
shoulder to lean against,
a wake-up kiss, plush words
I loved to stroke:
My husband. We.

You hung the portraits of your great-
grandparents from Stuttgart
over the sofa: boiled collar,
fashionable shawl. The yellow
shellac of marriage
coats our faces too.

We're like the neoclassical facade
on a post office. Every small town
has such a building.
Pillars forget they used to be
tree trunks, their sap congealed

into staying put. I can feel it
happening in every cell—that gradual
cooling and drying.
There is that other law of nature
which lets the dead thing stand.

MARCEL'S AT 11:00

A field of snow without a track on it.

I sit myself down in the swivel chair.
Mirror, scissors, comb.
A man's hand furrowing my wet hair.

TROMPE L'OEIL

The sun inflaming the horizon is really
below it already, refracted, the way
water in the pitcher bends and enlarges
the stems of the roses. A habit
of light. There's evening and then
in the morning we pull on
leftover feelings, stiff
with old sweat. *Good morning. Coffee?*
Years rise and set in the safety of
such decorum.
I feed the roses bleach from a dropper
to keep them red, stealing
a few inches of time from death—
let them stand one more day
in crystal. The violent
ghost of a sun persists.

REHEARSAL

Driving to the airport, we pass the equestrian
statue in the park: the plumed general
on his narrow plinth. It's not easy
to sit bronzed in the traffic, splendid
in every weather. From his horse
he watches the cars plunging toward the tunnel,
three hooves stuck in cement.

I'm practicing to leave you.
Each year I leave a little more
and you drive me. Our words echo
from an undeclared distance.
Where are the tickets? I ask
though it's late to be asking.

Now I'm on the plane, buckled in, watching
a Western. That man in the blue shirt
is you, I'd pick you out anywhere.
You're taking off your boots as the wagons
tie up for the night. I knew
you'd be home by now, even with the traffic.
You're looking straight at me. So much dust
on a long journey. Dust on your cheeks,
your forehead, your hair.
I almost reach out to brush it away.

COASTING

The placid stewardess explained crash landings.
Six exits. Be careful to secure your mask.
No one listened. Now, outside the window,
ranges of unshoveled cloud.

We're coasting at thirty-two thousand
on a slope of air.
15 B and C unfold skimpy blankets,
doze off like stoics in the snow.

A half-sun keeps trailing the plane. It's sunrise
or maybe sunset.
I'm wedged against the double window
with its bright beads of cold.

When the plane hits the runway,
the wing slats will swing up and the brakes
clatter like kettledrums.
Whatever we've stowed overhead will go

pitching forward. I want to
stay here, tucked in among strangers
hugging toy pillows
in the long white sky.

HOW THE LAST ACT BEGINS

"The trouble with you is you're not
loving enough." A drastic
summons, a trumpet of
hard last words.

I'm dry as a biscuit
but somehow a breast of mine
stiffens, unbuttons
and offers itself. Is that
what you want?

Now your body's in bed again, crying
that it can't fall asleep.
I forget what to feel, but I'll do
what I'm trained to do:
go barefoot, make the children
take off their shoes. You require
absolute silence.

The mind thinks *lemon* and the tongue
puckers. But what about the woman
who painted a tiger on the wall so real
it scared her out of the house?

I'm not making this up:
the three of us on tiptoe, the shades
down, the house darkened, and you
center-stage, wearing
that shiny black satin eye-mask.

DON'T TELL THE CHILDREN

I

Daddy's sad. Soon he'll be
happy again. A story I'm reading them
for the first time. Little spurts of
hot paint stain the page,
green spiky leaves.
They don't know the words yet.

I don't know the words.
I'm a child who has heard things
she shouldn't. Listening all night
at the grown-ups' door and I can't
make sense. Won't. I'm a child
hiding from my children.

2

Bedtime stories for the children:

The cheetah is the fastest land animal. It has tawny fur marked with black
spots. It is easily tamed. Giraffes are the tallest animals on earth. They eat
leaves from the tops of trees. Snails move very slowly. They carry their shell-
houses on their backs.

And for the grown-ups, an ancient tale:

The war horse says Ha! ha! among the trumpets. The eagle drinks blood.
The ostrich leaves her eggs in the dust. She forgets her young. The bones of
Behemoth are iron and brass. Leviathan churns the waters to a boil. His
nostrils are a caldron; his breath, flame.

3

The children sit on the rumpled blankets
and listen. They listen hard.
They're getting it all down
for future reference.

Tuned to our breath
they hear even the quarter tones.
They give off vibrations too keen for the ear,
like a struck tuning fork that goes on trembling.

CRESCENDO

The children, squabbling
in the back bedroom: *You started. No, you
started first.* I can hear him too
with his right to be angry, his fists
pounding on their door.

When they pause for a moment
the noise of the world rises:
cars spattering the gutters, rain
driven hard against the glass.
The wind is searching out flaws in the plaster.

Last night the children couldn't sleep.
If anything happens to you, they asked—
and stopped, because
this is the life I've caulked and grouted,
where else would they go?

Then that pounding again: *Let me in!*
I pull the drapes shut.
The stubborn din in the skull
doesn't make a sound.

CRAZED

We call glass *crazed* when it shatters like that.

The windshield of the car:
safety glass sculpted
by metal by fire by chance at eighty miles an hour
into swags of glittery spiderweb.

This time it was you, my love, my impossible,
who walked away from death.
Where are you headed so fast,
so lost?

Shards of glass on the dented hood, in the powdery
dust of the junkyard.
A burst of crystals on the totaled front seat.
Light spikes from the sharpest edge
and sharpens it.

I take a handful home in my pocket for luck.

In my desk drawer they turn into teeth
cusped and hungry,
the hard inside of a mouth.

THE EQUILIBRISTS

All year I've been trying to talk you
down from the ledge. Get down,
get down! I'll bring you hot milk and
rock you to sleep.

I'll put on my slingback heels, my red
lace nightie. Come, let me
unbutton your shirt, darling. What is it
you want?

Let's drive to Point Reyes, remember that
cabin out by the water,
there's an Italian movie you'll like
on Solano, how about a walk—

Think of the children! How can a father
of children
perch on a windowsill like a bird?

Here I am! you say, and lean forward
smiling, seductive:

What will you do now?

COMPOST

My hard carbuncular anger
scares me. This jackhammer rage.
Fever shakes me
till the whole house hurts. The heat
keeps building: peelings parings leaf-blades
blah blah of bright poison
bone meal and blood meal.

I want to stop him with one
annihilating word.
No, I won't say it. Let him
beg. Let him rise
on his hind legs and not get
the bone of an answer.

A soil of soils is breeding
in the smolder—a prize humus
to grow a marvel in,
some monstrous cabbage of a thousand leaves.
Oh my extravagant loam.
I shovel it under.

WHAT IT TAKES

A dream of sugar on the stairs.
It pools underfoot
and I slip on it. Every sweet
turns slippery. "Give me

a little hug," you say, and lie down
on the sofa. Then you get up
and go back to bed.

On the dresser, a crumpled glove
like a lung
with the air seeped out. On the bedspread
a shaft of acid sun.

Don't you see I can't touch you? My hands
are snipped at the wrist
and sewn back with flimsy thread.
I have to hold them perfectly still.

We're the stunned
couple in the Hopper painting.
The woman stares out the window.
If this is what it's like, she thinks,
I can take it.

ARCHIPELAGO OF DREAMS

Those long-stemmed glasses, islands where I drift
           in a viscous
     sea of unsleeping, doped
               on vodka and Benadryl,
  the book dizzy in my hands.

                Those glasses, crystal, a wedding gift
          from my brother. We used to wash them by hand
               and set them to dry on the striped towel.
      I want to show you an amazing thing:
             wine swirls and flames in a cracked glass
          and the glass doesn't break

              though fire, can you hear me? Fire
        is scorching the floorboards. *Help!*
              Get help! And you
     stand puzzled at the dream phone,
        fumbling the yellow pages.

  Then you're the hump of wet clay
       on my back. *It's dead, shake it off.*
Who said that? I didn't know
          that golem was you
    till it lay in a pine box, eyes so pale
      they were almost translucent.

        Tonight we're at the coast again, swimming,
          but we don't recognize each other.
   The waves sting. Then the tide comes in,
     our faces tilting the water
        like dazed icebergs.

MOTHER HUNGER

1

Every knothole was a branch once.

The way her face dissolved
that time she went away: *I have to go, I have to!*
His swollen *No, mama!* His wet
hands pulling
at her woolen skirt. He had to

stand there
stand there forever with the hired auntie and watch
as car after car of the long train
turned into steam.
Don't cry. You're a big boy now.

And then she was
back again, white-faced
mother of sorrows. A shriek at the window,
a worry on the shelf like a Meissen vase
a child mustn't break.

2

How the heat scatters her. A sudden whip
of wind. Here and there a bristly growth,
narrow leaves flinching.

They live in one close room,
a nest of flaking

newspapers. To have come
to this. Ten steps from bed
to dresser. Another five
to the door. And the child
clouding and polishing his face
in the family spoons.

Her child, after all. *You are my
everything,* she whispers,
and he nods.
Then that thirst rises in her—
                                She buries
her mouth in his cheek, his neck.

In the green bowl: heaped oranges,
the casual abundance of that other life.

3

Terrible always to be teetering
on stilts, those small wooden platforms
six inches off the ground.
He won't ever walk gracefully
though he is learning not to fall.

The applause that comes like a full stop
at the end of a sentence
is reward, or almost.
Still, he has to beg for it.

He wants to go down to the pond
after school like the others
and fish for tadpoles.
He'll take them home in a biscuit tin

with moss and water, a few twigs
to keep them company—
                          But there is papa
waving his arms again, shouting:
You must not worry mama.
And there is mama.

To live in their gaze
is to live in a house of glass.
Wherever he looks out
a severe love presses at the pane,
looking in.

4

The child a palimpsest of his parents'
losses, each one slapped over
the last—wet paint of
swastikas on the windows
of that two-hundred-year-old house
and the money the maid stole
to help them get out and mama's
But if we get caught?
Red *J* of the passports, stamped
in the sweat of their hands.

Then that land of promises where the heat
flays the houses
where grass burns to khaki dust in the sun
where papa pedals uphill and
falls off the bike
dead at ten in the morning
just because it's over doesn't mean
it stops happening

and mama's still a little Ida in pigtails
crying in the corner.

He raises a puzzled face for her
pitying kiss. She's waiting for him.
It's her grief that flashes across
his old night sky. His hands shake
as hers did the year she died, he can't
hold a glass or write
his name on the line. Her terror
grips him. He turns
the soiled pages of his book
with her clumsy wet thumb.

FOOLING THE ENEMY

His mouth twitches as he bends
to sign himself in.
"I'm getting better," he says.
"Do they know how sick I am?"

Every morning he'd slap on a frantic cheer
like an old woman
with gummy rouge on her cheeks
to fool the enemy.

Now his camouflage has been stripped away.
He holds a hand to his face
to cover his nakedness.

I don't know that gray-haired child.
Don't know that woman either, that wife
who sits dumbly beside him, under
her dropcloth of calm.

She's the one in disguise now,
a lizard that stiffens and pretends
to be tree bark. She won't move
even if you touch her
though panic—
panic goes on pulsing her throat.

STRAW BASKET

She goes there every day on the way home from work.
At the corner of Milvia and Dwight
she slows down to take in the blinking Emergency sign,
the barred windows, like a bank's.

She has to ring the buzzer of Third Floor East to get in.
She recites her name to the metal ear of the door,
the small round strainer of names.
That's how she remembers who she is.

He'll be sitting on his bed with the shades down,
his eyes double-locked.
She says his name once, twice, but nothing opens.
Then a feeble smile passes over his face.
He offers her a fish-kiss, scaly, moist.

Today he holds out a straw basket
with a bunch of red wooden cherries on the lid.
Sullen and proud. *For you.* He won't look up.
He's just finished winding the wire stems around the handle.
And says, the way their sons used to say,
I made this for you.

HERE

Anything
even the black
satin road where it catches
the streaked oils of stoplights
as I drive home alone
from the hospital
rain pocking the windshield
tires slicing the pooled water
to a spume taller than the car.
Even that patch where the road
fell in, rutted as a face, even that
cries out: Look at me
don't turn away, admit
the ravage is beautiful.
The world insists: I was here
before you and your pain,
I am here and I
will outlast you. *Yes,* says
the mind stroking itself
into life again
as a body, taking
what comfort
it can.

IN THE WARD

1

Soon nothing will be left but his *No*
that can't help itself,
can't stop, a phonograph needle
trailing a little clot of dust
that shudders when it touches down.

He sags on the bed till his face
falls into his hands.
Pitted gray pumice, moon-chalk
eroding into the acid air.

2

All year I dropped words into the well
of his silence. I could hear them
falling, could measure
the darkness they displaced.
I bent over the water and saw
my own face looking down.

Now he won't look at me.
He's watching the light
puddle on the floor: *I'm not listening.*

I hear a cave-sound
from inside him, a knucklebone scraping
an interior wall.

3

To the doctor he says,
"They take care of you in the hospital."

And then slowly, after a pause,
"I like
to be taken care of."

The doctor listens briskly, inspects
one shirt cuff, then the other, clean cotton
in a sheath of tweed.
Something starchy in him
crackles when he smiles.

4

Birds have eaten the breadcrumbs
and there is no moon.

Little hut in the forest,
how will I find you?

ECT

Electricity
scours his brain.
When they wheel him back
he has a just-wiped look on his face,
cool and shiny.
But where does the pain go?
The doctor wrings out the dishrag
and hangs it up to dry.

He can start over, revised,
an airbrushed photograph
with a girlish innocence around the eyes.
He's a tourist with only one shirt, and he's wearing it.
How light he feels.
He has dumped the cargo that made him founder,
the two-ton crates where rage
pounded in the nails.

"What's your name? Who's your wife?
Your children?"
His eyes flicker.
His new face, blank as an eggshell,
bobbles in the current.

VISITING HOURS ARE OVER

Down the hall past the half-
closed doors
a body
crumpled on every bed
striped pajamas three pills
in a pleated cup past the windows
double-glazed against
the cold past the waxy
sansevieria past the lead apron
of hospital drapes
down the front steps into rain
two blocks to the car
I run
just to feel
my feet
slap the
pavement my hands
slam against my sides
cold wet
cold slippery wet
I don't
open the umbrella

THE COLLECTOR

1

The Roxie is down the street from the locked ward
where I left my husband.
I took the children to the movies that night,
a comedy about the war.
In the candy dark, the laughs
went off like explosions. Here's the letter he left me,
a green crayon scrawl. These
are the sayings I tacked to the wall
and the meager patience
I lace myself into. Here's the Primo Levi I carry
in my pocket: only catastrophe
will calm me. And here's
the comfortable voice of my so-called friend:
You had it too good.

2

I collect what he does
the way other people save string.
Bottle-tops, trivets, bone buttons
with tag-ends of thread in them, gritty
loose change—
                    I don't know how to sort or let go
so I stash it all, rusted feelings
without handles or wheels.

And the brain with its gullet, its coiled gut,
its gripping, its kneading, its

squeezing-of-the-damp-out
all day and all night—

3

The *shlup-shlup* of his slippers
down the hall to the kitchen
where he rules by gag law: *Don't say that.*
I'm a sick man. It's not my fault.

Yes. He's home again.
I shake the dry pod of my heart
and pray for a twitch of feeling,
a little rattle of love.

His fist pounding my shoulder
demands absolution.
I'm allowed two sentences: *You're fine.*
You're going to be fine.

THE RULE OF GRAMMAR

The past tense is so severe,
it makes everything
smaller.

I love you, we said
to each other
like that moment in running when both feet
are off the ground.

CLEAR AND COLD

The leaves are brown paper bags.
What holds them to the tree
is a bit of twine.
I hate to say it, but I want them to fall.

I wanted my father to die when I knew
the doctors couldn't save him.
And I loved him.

I dreamed you were dead.
And I loved you. All that fury
of bloom when we started
unbuttoning, unzippering
singing *love, love,* to each other
sap rising in the trunk and streaming,
streaming in the branches.

Now we're sad twins
dressed in the same starched pinafores.
We sit all day on the porch and stay clean.
And I loved you. Loved you.
I sat at my father's bedside
and watched him go.

THE END OF SAFETY

1

The children have vanished
into the free fall
of sleep. Now the house is quiet
though it makes little settling noises.
I lock the front door
and turn off all the lamps but one,
my gooseneck
with its bare island of light.

I have a pencil, a yellow pad, a glass of water,
and a ring on the fourth finger of my left hand
that my right hand keeps
turning and turning.

2

How I loved the calm of self-stick triangular corners.
The soothing black pages. The ceremony
of choosing what to save. How safe I felt
those long winter afternoons when rain
lulled the roof
as I sorted and cropped—

You, woman, you with both faces to the past,
enough! Why keep insisting it was wrong,
all wrong,
from the beginning? You, with your

interest in history, look at the two of us
feeding each other popcorn in living color
like all true lovers. Or kissing
in the kitchen, the crazy apron
tied around us both. In this one, can't you see?
I hold up the baby as proof
in the flickering shadow of the live oak.

3

Safety: a strip of amber
hall light, insulation
under the door.

To live without looking, to be able
to lay your hand on
any cup on the shelf—

4

Do you love him? *Yes, I still love him.* Do you
love him? *No.*

Pain is carving me out so different
I can't go back. Not even if I want to

and I don't anymore.
What I have now

is who I am,
down to the bare worked wood.

And yet, says my hand-in-the-cupboard self. *And yet.*

5

Winter morning picks out the bare
branches of the fig tree: a thin-lipped
unblinking light.
I sit in the ladder chair without moving.

A smudge like an oily thumbprint
where a bird bruised the glass.
Where was it flying so possessed with air and light
before it fell?

THOUGH YOU HAVEN'T ASKED

Because stones grow in the belly
like fists of salt—

Because the screen door keeps scraping,
swollen,
and won't stay closed—

Because the scar in the treebark
is larger every year—

Because you sit in the corner
and sulk—

I work the ring off and rub
my naked finger.

The ring's in my pocket.

Something is rolling downhill fast
gathering speed.

BEFORE

This is the moment before the petals
drift to the tabletop.
The roses are open now, drooping

from their own spent weight.
He has backed into a corner, one hand
caught in a pocket, one hand across his chest

as if to defend himself. He brought her
the roses out of habit
or helplessness, which he calls

love: blown roses on impossible
spindle stems. Her eyes waver
as she turns away.

She hasn't told him yet
and he waits head down, though
he knows already.

Each time they speak, the words
open a little more heavily
on their stems.

A HIGH WIND

rages in the house tearing sheets
from the mirrors slipcovers
from the chairs stripping
everything naked.
Lightning flares at the windows
zinc-white. All the sluices open.

A rack of branches on the sidewalk
like broken antlers. Only joy
with its floods
and fires
could be so cleansing.

I want to be out in this wind that can drive
a nail through a tree trunk. Let the
dead wood fall!
There is still time to say what the two of us
never dared—

Let it bring the house down.

THE KISS

There was a ghost at our wedding,
the caterer's son,
who drowned that day.

Like every bride I was dressed
in hope so sharp
it tore open
my tight-sewn fear.

You kissed me under the wedding canopy,
a kiss that lasted a few beats longer
than the usual,
and we all laughed.

We were promising: the future
would be like the present,
even better, maybe.
Then your heel came down
on the glass.

We poured champagne
and opened the doors to the garden
and danced
a little drunk, all of us,

as the caterer made the first cut,
one firm stroke, then
dipped his knifeblade
in the water.

blood honey

AUTUMN HOUSE PRESS, 2009

THE NEW WORLD

My uncle killed a man and was proud of it.
Some punk with a knife came at him in Flatbush
and he knocked the sucker to the ground.
The sidewalk finished the job.

By then he'd survived two wives
and a triple bypass. He carried
a bit of the plastic tubing in his pocket
and would show it to anyone.
He'd unbutton his shirt right there on the street
and show off the scar.

As a boy, he watched a drunken Cossack
go after his father with an ax.
His sister tried to staunch the bleeding
with a hunk of dry bread.

That's the old country for you:
they ate with their hands, went hungry to bed,
slept in their stink. When pain knocked,
they opened the door.

The bitter drive to Brooklyn every Sunday
when I was a child—
Uncle George in the doorway snorting and laughing,
I'm gonna take a bite of your little behind.

He was a good-looker in a pin-striped suit
and wingtip shoes.
*This is America, we don't live
in the Dark Ages anymore, honey.
This is a free country.*

TELL ME

Tell me the story where you hit your father.
I've heard it, but tell me again
how he'd come after you when he'd had too many,
how one day finally
you gave him what he asked for
and there he was—flat
on the kitchen floor.

You put the door behind you and started walking.
Your legs kept you moving from one block to the next
while the drone in your blood
mulled it over.

When you got back at midnight, your father
kept his mouth shut. You too.
The words that slept in that house
were homeless and hungry.
You had all learned to step around them.

Tell me that story. I wait for the part where
your whole hand
pronounces a single word
so unmistakable
there's no way to take it back.
It's a story from hell
but I like it. Lie down with me, love,
and tell it from the beginning.

POTATO EATERS

My grandmother never did learn to write.
"Making love" was not in her lexicon;
I wonder if she ever took off her clothes
when her husband performed his conjugal duties.
She said God was watching,
reciting Psalms was dependable medicine,
a woman in pants an abomination.

In their hut on the Dniester
six children scraped the daily potatoes from a single plate;
each one held a bare spoon.

Five years from the shtetl her daughters
disguise themselves
in lisle stockings and flapper dresses.
The boys slick their hair with pomade.
What do they remember of Russia? "Mud."

That's grandma in the center. At ease in owl glasses.
Don't run, you'll fall.
Mostly she keeps her mouth shut; the children
would rather not hear.
What does a full stomach know
of an empty stomach?

It's time you opened your mouth, bobbe;
I'm old enough now to ask you a thing or two
and you're too dead to be annoyed.
You'll know where to find me,
I'm the daughter of your second son.
I have the spoons.

BROTHERS

When I was the Baba Yaga of the house
on my terrible chicken legs,
the children sat close on the sofa as I read,
both of them together
determined to be scared.

Careful! I cackled, stalking them
among the pillows:
You bad Russian boy,
I eat you up!
They shivered and squirmed, my delicious sons,

waiting for a mighty arm
to seize them.
I chased them screeching down the hall,
I catch you, I eat you!
my witch-blade hungry for the spurt
of laughter—

        What stopped me
even as I lifted my hand?
The stricken voice that cried: *Eat him!*
Eat my brother.

THE MESSIAH OF HARVARD SQUARE

Every year some student would claim to be the Messiah.
It was the rabbi who had to deal with them.
He had jumped, years ago, from a moving boxcar
on the way to a death camp. That leap
left him ready for anything.

This year at Pesach, a Jewish student proclaimed
Armageddon. "Burn the books! Burn the textbooks!"
he shouted to a cheerful crowd,
sang Hebrew songs to confuse the Gentiles,
dressed for the end like Belshazzar.
People stopped to whisper and laugh.
"I have a noble task," the boy explained.
"I must prepare myself to endure
the laughter of fools."

The rabbi was a skeptic.
Years ago he'd been taught: If you're planting a tree
and someone cries out, *The Messiah has come!*
finish planting the tree. Then
go see if it's true.

Still, he took the boy into his study
and questioned him meticulously,
as if the poor soul before him might be,
God help us, the Messiah.

REPRIEVE

We were drinking coffee in her pre-war flat,
four walls, Pompeiian gray
to match her complexion.
An old Jewish woman in Prague.
Her dead husband laughing in a dapper suit,
fedora, cigarette, one arm around a life
flash-frozen and set at the table
beside the Czech pastries.

She held me with her skinny hand.
"I could have left after the war with my baby
and started over." And then,
half to herself: "Did I make a mistake?"
Her baby was translating
into a broken German I could manage.

What a question to ask a green girl like me,
still too married to regret a marriage
I thought I chose.
Still three or four wars away from knowing
when a question
isn't a question, just a gasp of loss—
but mine to translate.

She poured coffee, passed the kolacky, awaited
my verdict. *Yes, you should have left.*
No, you did the right thing.

As if I could reprieve a life
by pointing a finger
left or right.

FLOUR AND ASH

for Gale Antokal

Today she is working in seven shades of gray.

She tacks a sheet of paper to the wall,
primes her palette with flour and ash,
applies the fine soft powders with a fingertip,
blending with her thumb.

"Make flour into dough," she tells me,
"and fire will turn it into food.
Ash is the final abstraction of matter.
You can just brush it away."

Day lilies in the flush of summer-
about-to-be-fall. Her garden burns
red and yellow in the dry August air
and is not consumed.

On her studio wall, a heavy
particulate smoke
thickens and rises. Footprints grime the snow.
The about-to-be-dead line up on the ramp
with their boxy suitcases,
ashen shoes.

She hovers over her creation
as if she too has a mind
to brush against it
and wipe it out.

COVENANT

in memory of Paul Celan

What he was given was too hot to touch.
Live coal, glowing from the altar.

He took it
in the tongs of metaphor
so it wouldn't burn.

But it did burn. He reached for it
anyway. Slowly, slowly.

His poems are a miracle
of perversity. They knew before he did
what words give

and words take away.
How they slake
and inflame. How they salt
every morsel they save.

He left a place at the table
for the silence
that pressed a burning coal
to his lips.

POWER

"Why can't they just get along?" he protests
when he hears the numbers on the morning news.
Then he's got the answer:
"They're people, that's why."

Thus saith my neighbor
who lets his Doberman out to bark at midnight
and grumbles, "Yeah, yeah"
when I call to complain.

Meanwhile, in the precincts of power,
the new Chief of Staff
who learned his trade as a fighter pilot
is fending off questions from his swivel chair.

"And what did you feel," the reporters ask,
"when you dropped a bomb from an F-16?"
I felt a slight lift of the wing, he says.
After a second it passed.

THE SPOILS

The mother of Sisera cried through the lattice,
Why is his chariot so long in coming?
                              —Judges 5:28

An Israeli soldier, just back from the '67 war,
gave me a photo he found of a mother and son,
a talisman the enemy wore to battle
in his khaki shirt pocket.

What was he offering me that day
—a trophy? a souvenir?
I didn't ask and he answered:
all he wanted was to get home safe.

His mother, my neighbor, fought the war
cigarette by cigarette
in a Jerusalem shelter,
clinging to the phone like Sisera's mother.

Home safe, he let me take
a shot of him holding his dazed mother,
a shot of him cradling his gun.

Then he gave me the photo he found
in a dead man's pocket
and without thinking I took that too.

THE COLORS OF DARKNESS

Rothko Chapel, Houston

Flash after flash across the horizon:
tourists trying to take the Grand Canyon
by night. They don't know
every last shot will turn out black.

It takes Rothko sixty years to arrive
at the rim of his canyon.
He goes there only after dark.
As he stands at the railing, his pupils open
like a camera shutter at the slowest speed.

He has to be patient. He has to lean
far over the railing
to see the colors of darkness:
purple, numb brown, mud red, mauve
—an abyss of bruises.
At first, you'd think it was black-on-black.
"Something you don't want to look at," he says.

As he waits,
the colors vibrate in the chasm
like voices:
                    You there with the eyes,
bring back something from
the brink of nothing
to make us see.

THE DEAD OF NIGHT

An old memory comes home
in new clothing
at the dead of night,

turns a cold key in the lock.
A whiff
of camphor and Chanel.

Settles down in my best chair,
Don't let me disturb you,
and stakes its claim.

An old shame forgets what it came for.
An old fear scatters salt.
A young loss waits at the window.

An old grief whimpers and a new grief
kisses it. An intimate anger
takes off its clothes.

BEQUEST

If only you were my father, the child says
to his mother's lover.
A contrary-to-fact clause. The child
is hardly a child, he's twenty-five,
old enough to know the grammar
of second-guessing.

He's got to rake his way
through all the dead lives. With his sleeve
he wipes the sweat from his brow.

Imagine, once
our mothers and fathers were strangers
to each other! How strange they are.
One hangs over the changing table
clucking and cooing,
one waves a little scepter that rattles.

They hover like a muggy sky.
Then the wind picks up
and their dust clings to us, a habit
there's no shaking off.

MIRROR, MIRROR

The body in the bedroom mirror
is my mother's,
the one I found so hopeless
when I was fifteen.

She was undressing; I was trying on
her satin, chiffon, gold lamé
America. One size too small.

A bookish girl from Russia she called me
when I swore off lipstick.
Books don't know everything.
Stand up straight. Tie your hair back.
Don't give me that look.

On my dresser, a photo of her at seventy,
tilting her head, leaning out of the frame
—the better to see my life?
Her assessor's eye is shrewd but genial.

Things are easier between us lately.
One would almost think death
has mellowed her—

                    Or has it?
She has something to tell me
but she's taking
her own sweet time.

SWEEPING UP

The war is over now, and the field
lies in a litter of aftermath
—teacup and tablecloth,
Nitrostat, lipstick, the new Danielle Steel,
your misspelled DO NOT RESOSITATE,
the ordinary disorder.
I am your custodian. You have left me
to sweep up the leavings.

I've given the sofa away but the dishes
are still in my basement, the rosebud china
I'll never use. Your letters are fading
in the interrogative light of day
that bleaches everything it touches.

Tell me, mother, that amber ring
you bestowed with such solemnity,
did you know it was glass?
What if we'd talked about the life after
tea-and-mandelbroyt,
where would that have taken us?
Did you ever find out if I was your child?

Your floral nightgown,
the one you hemmed in a hurry
with crooked stitches
—it fits. I'll admit: I keep wearing it.
I keep choosing to wear it.

What have you taken with you
that I might have used?

THE DISCIPLINE OF MARRIAGE

My mother said what she thought.
If my father looked up from the paper to inquire
where the hell anyone would get such a dumb idea,
she'd reply, with a smile like a warning:
"That's how I feel."

Her feelings were larger than his,
full of grievance, of steaming griefs.
She hung up her keys at the door
and salted the daily stew.

All day my father depleted his poor stock of words.
Evenings he shrank and fell silent.
The discipline of marriage had taught him
every last thing he knew about silence
and its rewards. After supper, he'd shut his eyes,
park his feet on the hassock and kiss
the evening goodbye.

My mother applied glittery blue to her eyelids.
Crystal bottles commanded her dressing table
with their flags of milky glass;
the French perfumes glowed like topaz.
She had plenty to say. She wanted him
to listen, to say something back! Open
his eyes for once and see her!
Her beaded purse! Her alligator shoes!

THE DARK OF DAY

We were trying to keep things neat and shiny.
Twenty-four years.
We had two sets of dishes—one for love,
one for hate. We kept them in separate cupboards.
Eat love and hate at the same meal
and you'll get punished.

The rabbis taught us the mathematics of dividing
this from that. They certified
the micro-moment when day tips over
into night: *When the third star presents itself in the sky.*
They drew a line through that eye of light, a longitude.
You've got to navigate the evening blessing
with precision, not one star too soon.
But night comes on slowly.
It takes all day.

My friend's father was killed
in a car crash. She hated him,
hadn't seen him in years.
When the police called, she drove to the ditch
where his wrecked Chevy waited for the tow-truck.

The body was gone. On the dashboard, broken glasses,
an open notebook splotched with his blood.
Then she was crying, not knowing why.
She tore out a stain on the mottled paper,
his ragged last breath,
and took it into her mouth.

WILD HONEY

A puddle of sun on the wooden floor.
The infant crawls to it, licks it,
dips a hand in and out, out and in,
letting the wild honey
trickle through his fingers.

Then that voice from on high,
Look at the pretty color!
wipes up the glory with a rag of language.

THROUGH A GLASS

On the crown of his head
where the fontanelle pulsed
between spongy bones,
a bald spot is forming, globed and sleek
as a monk's tonsure.

I was the earliest pinch of civilization,
I was the one who laced him
into shoe leather
when he stumbled into walking upright.
"Shoes are unfair to children," he'd sulk.

Through a pane of glass
that shivers when the wind kicks up
I watch my son walk away.

He's out the door, up the street, around
a couple of corners by now.
I'm in for life.
He trips; my hand flies out—

I yank it back.

BLUE

The sky isn't really blue, it just looks blue
the way we looked happy in the family album.

So the grass isn't green either?
No, the grass is green,
or green enough in California
till summer burns it brown.
We call that *gold*.

And paper is white until it turns brittle.
What an odd compulsion, to preserve
the remains of the day
on paper. Paper!
When I turn the pages, bits of the old life
flake off in my hands,

a few worn hopes without punctuation
I once called *love*
as I lurched
from one hope to the next, irremediably
deep in blue.

Who could be happy in a life like that?
I was. It's true.
The *real* truth, as we say, to distinguish it
from the other one.

NATURAL HISTORY

It takes a long time to make a meadow.
First you need glaciers
to gouge out a lake.
Then reeds grow, the lake fills with silt
and eventually grass.

How many trees with their litter
of fallen leaves to beget
a single live joy?
Look at the dead ends
up and down that trunk. Each one
could have been a branch.

How many miles between heart
and mouth.
     And the words fall
like belated raindrops
the day after a storm when you shake the tree,
if you happen to shake it.

THE REMAINS

It's not the heat of his body
unhesitating
under the apricot tree, but the pack of cigarettes
crushed in his front pocket.

Not his girlfriend's so-nicely-phrased advice,
but the jiggly necklace of pencil stubs
she liked to wear.

Once again an inferior memory
has been installed, in place of
the one you could actually use.
You don't get to choose your dreams either.

And the past you severed and tossed
that messy afternoon
is still yours, conferred in perpetuity,
cramped and throbbing
like a phantom limb.

Sometimes you're tempted to kick
just to make sure it's no longer there.
Of course it's no longer there.
No reason why it should go on hurting.

A LITTLE NIGHT MUSIC

We don't know each other. That's the best part.
That we won't meet again
is almost as good.

The sky is moonless—so close
we can reach up to adjust
the overhead stars.

It's quiet, except for the weary
drone of a world
that has someplace to go

and follows its nose straight to the landing strip.
Let it rumble along in its sleep;
we can stay up all night!

We have no route map,
no carry-ons,
no turbulence,

just the easy skies of Laissez-Passer
and our naked lives.
What a pleasure to meet

in the spacious intimacy
of strangers
before shame is invented.

PRIVATE LIVES

I know a man who is always performing.
He has a limited repertoire.
If I ask, "Where are you going?"
he'll produce a smile
slick as a handshake.

His face is fully dressed
but his wife's face is stripped
to bone and pain.
Whatever that man is trying to hide
the nakedness of her face uncovers.

When the living room lights come on,
their private life is projected,
cropped by the window frame,
on a public screen.

Once my life too was Top Secret
common knowledge.
Strangers would season their day with my sorrows.
I was the salt of their evening meal.

Now it's my turn. I ought to say
Pull the shades! Don't let me see!
Instead I stand for as long as the moment lasts
in the comfortable dark,
letting the inside
look out.

SALVAGE

The master's asleep in his chair, his snore
a shrill trapped wind in the narrow hallway.
And on the bathroom sink, a pink-and-white
half-moon smile in a glass of water.
All night the smile persists
apart from him.

The nattering of clock, fridge, traffic, even
his creaky rocker—the world is getting louder.
At dinner he clicks his hearing aid
down into the ashtray.
Another door shut.

But the silence, isn't it oppressive?
I can't hear you, he answers agreeably.
Each age has its privileges.

I'm ready to go, he's been saying.
We have all heard him say it.
But in the torpor of four o'clock
he was mending a threadbare pillowcase
on the back porch today.
A few stitches will do it.

How can he leave? There are still
three soap-ends he glued into one
in the broken soap dish.
Under the hard hot rush of the faucet
it dwindles steadily in his hands.

A MANTLE

What she wants these days is to hurt
the world back. Bereavement
may keep her warm
and it's hers to wear as she bears him

into each day's cold.
Let a living man sing what he pleases,
a wife inherits
riddles and a stone. Grief

can be quarried and polished,
loss can be coined.
A widow is a bride of darkness,
like it or not.

She likes it. When he lived
she was smaller. Now she assumes
the great man's coat as though
she'd wrought it. Her anger at last
has found its calling.

THE NAKED FUTURE

We were sitting on my sofa with his dead wife.
(A good-looking woman, he allowed.)
All those women who wanted him.

On the sofa I saw a soldier of love
strutting his wounds and badges.
And what did he see?
I was tired of the future already, and we hadn't
started yet. We hadn't even started.

Sex is a brisk new broom. Tough, efficient.
It knows all the corners.

And that's how, one autumn evening, we began
dropping this-and-that onto the drafty floor
—history with its pockets, ticket-stubs, torn seams,
husbands and wives. He slipped off my watch
and laughed, "Oh, come on,"
when I stopped to pick up his blue shirt
and smooth it over the chair.

Then that implacable broom swept us bare.

PORTRAIT OF THE ARTIST

He showed me the painting he made of me
—at eighty? ninety? Clearly
he didn't mean to flatter.
Now he asks if I'm planning to write
a poem about him. He's smiling,
but under that brushed-on smile
he looks worried.

There's a couple of things he'd prefer to spare
the reading public.
Who wants to be published
stripped to his cotton socks,
with nothing but a fig leaf of metaphor
to keep him decent?

Sweetie, it's not you in the poem—it's you
ground to grist and pigment
with all the others. Don't you know
what a poet can do with a blank
sheet of paper? Words
are the poor man's colors.

Listen, I promise: I'll change your name.
And I'll never ask you to pose
legs crossed, eyes bright, cheek nuzzling
your hand—*Don't move! So I can get you
just like that.* Move all you want, I'll
get you, I've been getting you
all along.

A LONG WINTER'S NIGHT

The hands
are the hands of a young man making love
but his voice is parched. *I want to be*
myself again.

To be himself.
The way an old tree is green again
after the winter.
The way a tree that's cut down will bud
at the scent of water.

His hands are the hands of a lover.
When I see him drop them to cover himself
I understand winter and trees and bolts
on the inside of doors.

How can a woman understand? he asks
with blind hands
groping for green. I never saw
a man so naked.

ROSH HASHANA

I start the new year by emptying my pockets
off the bridge in Live Oak Park.
Tashlich. Another year of crumbs.

Old sticky rancors I feed on in secret,
wadded tissues, *he saids* and *I saids*,
snarled hair, lint:
Let the water take it!

What a muddle we make,
I with my swagger of *This time I mean it*,
all the while thinking *Maybe.*
My right hand on the doorknob, resolute,
and the left
ready to warm itself in his pocket
till the end of days.

This time I mean it. As the bridge is my witness
and the water
under the bridge

and hard by the water, the snake
with its castoff story, its body stocking
sloughed in the dirt.

LIVING WITH MYSELVES

They're up at all hours, the two of them,
sorting, pressing and folding
as they bundle the daily wash
in a plain gray wrapper.
They're always losing something.
What they deliver is full of holes,
I'm not sure it's even mine.

The left doesn't know what the right is doing.
One has a heart; one does the chores.
When things get tough, I hear them go at it:
"I can't live with that." "I can."

But on the nights when they're screening
the dream of the secret room,
I'm ready to forgive everything.
"A room in hiding! Right in our house!"
"Oh yeah. What else is new."

Each time the dream is different.
Louvered windows and a bare wooden floor
or a plush carpet with the luster of opal
—is that room dreaming me?
A doorknob slides into my hand
and the house starts to grow.

"This is the life you haven't lived,"
says the prickly one.
"This is your life," says the other. "It's time
you had a look around."

THE COLOR GREEN

in memory of Mark O'Brien

Two floors up, at the corner of Hearst and Shattuck,
he's clamped for good
in an iron lung. When it's time to eat
he inches his head a sweaty mile
to the edge of the pillow. It takes a while.

His brilliant bloodshot light-blue eyes
steer me from cupboard to fridge:
he would like his chicken burrito
cut into bite-size pieces,
a bent straw for his glass of water, please.

How does the body live its only life
in a cage? I watch him compute the distance
from bar to bar, and squeeze
between them
with a violent compression, a fury of bursting free
that doesn't last.

His will is a crowbar, angled to pry up
the rooted intractable weight
of matter. I watch him slyly, I check out
the way he does it. He
does it. But pain in its absolute privacy
weighs what it weighs.

I come here to study the soul, posing one question
a dozen ways, most of them silent.
If I'm only a body, he laughs,

I'm up shit creek. His laugh
a gritty eruption of rock, salt and breath.

Like me he writes poems
but he does it letter by letter
on a propped keyboard, the mouth-stick
wobbling between his teeth.
That kind of speed keeps a poet accountable.
He won't ever say *The grass is very green*
when it's only green.

THE SIXTH AGE

Words slip from me lately
like cups and saucers
from soapy hands.
I grope for the names of things
that are governed, like me, by the laws
of slippage and breakage.

I am like a child
left behind by the fast-talking
grownups. A tourist
lost in the blind alleys
of a foreign language.

How will I see my way to anywhere
without my words?

I slam up and down the stairs of our house:
Where are my glasses hiding?
Rimless, invisible as oxygen.
I need glasses to find them.

There must be words left
to go on searching for the ones I've lost

the way the blind man I once loved
found me,
first with his fingertips,
then with his whole hand.

A BURIED LANGUAGE

"If you catch it early—." The nurse
plucked a thorn from the air,
then pressed a solemn palm to her breast
like pledging allegiance.

She was teaching my hand to read
a buried language, to grope
for a knot of consonants tough as gristle.
"Armpit to bra line, sternum
to collarbone."

Each month again
steam fills the shower; my hand
slips into its glove of soap.

You must do this, my mind
instructs the hand that feeds me,

but each month again my hand,
my capable good right hand
that could save me,

backs away.

THE BULLET

passed through her brain at an acute angle
and lodged in the soft tissue
of our lives.

It was then we knew her,
mantle and magma.

Last Tuesday, in a plaid suit, she looked
—what did we call it, *happy?*
Though strictly speaking, she was invisible.

Now, in the searchlight of her death,
I can make out
her hand, her fingers, the barrel clamped
between her teeth. I can taste it,
that bulking metal. It makes me gag.

I go on arguing with her back.
How easy it is, she answers
without turning. *A click of the finger,
a puff of smoke.*

                              Grief
is a strange anger. I want to grab her, twist
her trigger arm
hard.

ENVY

"Damned if I don't fight," Naomi swore
and I envied the way she said it.

She wanted to run downstairs,
pare an apple, dip her spoon in the sauce.
Wipe her own ass
and tie her shoelaces.
She was planning the battle from her hospital bed.
And I, of sound body and greedy heart—
I envied the way she said it.

Then she died and became available to us.
After the funeral we took
her life in our hands,
unraveled it.

A week ago she was reaching
for a bottle of Jean Naté, citron yellow,
beside a tumbler of purple asters,
a little still life on the bedside table.
"Would you rub my shoulders with cologne."

I swabbed her with long sweet lemon strokes,
a ritual washing of the body
this side of death.
When I finished, she looked almost happy.
By then she had only a few wishes left,
each one smaller than the last.

BLOOD HONEY

in memory of Amichai Kronfeld

Apprehended and held without trial,
our friend was sentenced:
brain tumor, malignant.
Condemned each day
to wake and remember.

Overnight a wall sprang up around him
leaving the rest of us
outside.

Death passed over us this time.
We're still at large. We're free
to get out of bed, start the coffee,
open the blinds.
The first of the human freedoms.

If he's guilty
we must be guilty; we're all made of
the same cup of dust—

It's a blessing, isn't it? To be able,
days at a time,
to forget what we are.

*

Today we have brunch at Chester's,
poached egg on toast,
orange juice foaming in frosted glasses.

He remembers the summer he packed blood oranges,
stripped to the waist,
drinking the fresh-squeezed juice in the factory
straight from the tap.
He cups his left hand under his chin
as if to a faucet, laughing.

He is scooping sweetness from the belly of death
—honey from the lion's carcass.

What is it, this blood honey?

⋆

A shadow is eating the sun.
It can blind you
but he's looking right at it,
he won't turn away.

Already his gaze is marked
by such hard looking.

Day after day breaks
and gives him
back to us
broken.

Soon the husk of his knowing
won't know even that.

⋆

A man lies alone in his body in a world
he can still desire.
Another slice of pie? he asks.

As long as he's hungry
he's still one of us.
Oh Lord, not yet.

He drums out a jazz beat on the bedrail
with his one good hand
when the words stumble.
See? he says. *I can trick the tumor.*

He can still taste and see.
The world is good.

He hauls himself up in bed,
squinting his one good eye at the kingdom
through a keyhole
that keeps getting smaller
and smaller.
It is good. It is very good.

THE KNOWN FACTS

You wake to the sloped ceiling,
to bedclothes steeped in moonlight.
If you start looking out the window now,
forget about sleep.

The known facts about him
are stones in a stream; it's the way you proceed
from here to there.
In the moonlight of your imaginings
the stones are slippery.

Other women have lifted their skirts
to stumble across, and you don't know
their story, either.

The unknown facts have dominion
over night and day.
Have you already managed to forget?

That force of gravity
governed your sky, its exploding stars,
a mass of dark matter
no one could see.

ON THE SHORTEST DAY OF THE YEAR

I love the bare trees that let me see them.
In winter I know what they are,
the articulation of the branches
down to the smallest twig.

Let the frozen pond
keep its secrets to itself.
The trees are open, full of sky, the forest
finally visible—

I can see past the pillars of sepia and snow,
past the fallen deadwood,
deep into the thicket.

That's how I want to know you,
in that clear light.

THE CUNNING OF HUNGER

A fox is worrying the wild turkeys in the meadow.
At last count one hen, nine chicks and a fox.
I've seen the chicks line up sweetly
to cross the meadow,
the fox a red-tailed streak in the grass.
The cunning of hunger makes him almost invisible.

You are way out of reach. Which leaves me
to brood about lust,
how it streaks from seeing to eating,

and the slow monotonous grind that sharpens
lust from a distance. How the body
has a mind of its own. How hunger
outfoxes our nimble plans.

Wherever you are, be warned:
across a few thousand fields of standing grass
I am setting out now, *now*,
to devour you.

SOMETIMES I WANT TO SINK INTO YOUR BODY

Sometimes I want to sink into your body
with the fever that spikes inside me
to be a woman
who can open a man.

Why must I be only softness and haunches,
a satin cul-de-sac?

You ought to know what sharpens me
like a barbed arrow.
Do you think we're so different?

How you tease me, twiddle me,
hustle me along,
just when I'd like to splay you
tooth and nail.

AFTER SEX

A man after sex
has that squishy thing in the nest of his lap.
A bashful appendage
like a Claes Oldenburg vinyl drainpipe,
a soft saxophone that won't toot a note.

A man's got to wear his susceptibility
out in plain sight.
No wonder he's keeping his soul
zippered up.

A woman's got that rock of a belly,
that baby cave,
breasts swaggering erect
when they swell with milk.
Oh she knows what it's like to sing
the stand-up song of a man.

Now you and I soften in the wash,
the body elastic goes slack.
We see ourselves in each other,
we grow alike.
We want to curl up in a sunny corner
and doze like the cat.

Come, flick a whisker,
make me remember.

VENI VIDI

Bellagio, Italy

The streets are still empty.
Behind metal shutters
the shops are getting a fresh coat of paint.

Even the weather isn't ready:
unseasonable frost,
though the greens of spring are beginning
to test the hardpan of winter.

In the piazza there's a single palm tree,
gawky as Big Bird,
its fronds wrapped in a canvas bustle,
one green tuft poking up like a tail.
It's being groomed for the season.
Any day now they'll let it out.

We're leaving on the next ferry
but we have time
to dash off a *Veni vidi*:

What a life! The tourist sign,
THIS WAY TO THE SUNSET,
the falconer, bird-in-hand,
the lake with its fresh coat of light.

THE SIXTH TRUMPET

after Anselm Kiefer

Lately we've begun to talk logistics,
to draw up contingency plans
for a war we're preparing
to lose. We're counting backwards

from D-day. *If I die first*, we tell each other.
Sometimes: *If you die first*. Declarations
flare in the street, the museum.
Our children can't stand that kind of talk,

they announce in front of Kiefer's painting.
They see an immense plowed field
under a day sky seeded with dark stars.
Sunflower seeds! they say. *He used real seeds.*

We see a bombardment of cinders
that fall through the air onto furrows
of emulsion, acrylic, shellac
to converge on a vanishing point.

No place to hide from the sky
—we'd better prepare a shelter
for them. We dole out small truths,
sufficient unto the day.

Sunflower seeds, we say.

TAKING THE TUG OF IT

Bury me in that cemetery on Fairmount
across from Fat Apple's,
where deer come to eat the flowers of the newly dead,
reds and yellows fresh from the florist.
A buck takes a whole bouquet in his mouth,
then gazes steadily at me.

It's a royal park—live oak, eucalyptus, pine—
with a view of two bridges and the Bay.
I like to walk in the presence of the dead.
It clears my mind.

★

An adult heart is the size of a fist.

And what does the heart do?
Hoists itself up each morning into the weather.
A fist is not just a sign of defiance:
four fingers and a thumb can grasp. And hold.

And what does the heart hold in that tight little fist?
The string of its one life on earth,
taking the tug of it, letting it fly,
not letting it fly away.

★

A dribble of dirt, of clods on wood.
The shovel passed hand-to-hand,

the coffin lid
a shiny door we were pelting shut.

I took home the hard
percussive thud.

⁎

Last time we talked about the afterlife,
we ended up snapping: "Arrogance!"
"Ignorance!" "Wishful thinking!"

Someday, I'll be a little pile of dust,
said Elihu to Job
with his sour smile. *And you'll be
a beam of light.*

ACKNOWLEDGMENTS

Many thanks to the editors of the following journals where the new poems first appeared, some in different versions or with different titles: *Beloit Poetry Journal, Catamaran, Coal Hill Review, Connotation Press, The Cortland Review, Field, The Kenyon Review, Literary Imagination, The Manhattan Review, The New Republic, Pleaides, Poet Lore, Prairie Schooner, Salmagundi, Southern Poetry Review, Southern Review, Spillway, Talking Writing, Valparaiso Poetry Review,* and *The Women's Review of Books.*

I owe the phrase "welter and waste" in "The Revised Version" to Robert Alter's translation of *tohu wa-bohu* (Genesis 1:2) in *The Five Books of Moses.*

I am grateful to the Sheep Meadow Press for permission to reprint poems from *The Secrets of the Tribe* and *The Past Keeps Changing,* to the University of Wisconsin Press for *Mrs. Dumpty,* and to Autumn House Press for *Blood Honey.*

My heartfelt appreciation to the Rockefeller Foundation's Bellagio Center, the Djerassi Resident Artists Program, Hedgebrook, the MacDowell Colony, and Yaddo. Much of this book was written or revised during residencies in those beautiful communities of writers and artists.

Deepest gratitude to my dear family and friends for their incisive criticism of my poems over many years, and for their sustenance during a particularly challenging time. To my sons Benjamin, psychologist and poet, and Jonathan, scientist and artist, whose insights I always value. To my accomplice-in-translation and sister-in-poetry, Chana Kronfeld. To my editors, Michael Simms and Giuliana Certo, for their generous support and meticulous attention to detail. To Chiquita Babb, for her elegant book design. To Donna Brookman, whose luminous painting *fullflood* graces the front cover. And most of all to Dave Sutter, my husband, who at twenty wrote prophetically, "Love is the youth we hunger for."

ABOUT THE AUTHOR

CHANA BLOCH, the author of award-winning books of poetry, translation and scholarship, is Professor Emerita of English at Mills College, where she taught for over thirty years and directed the Creative Writing Program. From 2007-2012 she served as the first poetry editor of *Persimmon Tree*, www .persimmontree.org, an online journal of the arts by women over sixty.

Her poetry has appeared in *The Atlantic Monthly, The Nation, The New Yorker, The Iowa Review, Poetry, Ploughshares, Threepenny Review*, and many other journals. It has been reprinted in *The Addison Street Anthology, American Poets Against the War, The Autumn House Anthology of Contemporary American Poetry, Best American Poetry, Chapter and Verse, Don't Leave Hungry, The Extra-ordinary Tide, The Face of Poetry, Jewish in America, Living in Storms, Living in the Land of Limbo, The Place That Inhabits Us, Pushcart Prize* VI and XXIX, *When She Named Fire*, and other anthologies.

Bloch is co-translator from Hebrew of *The Song of Songs, The Selected Poetry of Yehuda Amichai* and his *Open Closed Open*, and *Hovering at a Low Altitude: The Collected Poetry of Dahlia Ravikovitch*, and translator of Yiddish poetry and prose by Jacob Glatstein, Abraham Sutzkever, and Isaac Bashevis Singer. She is also the author of a scholarly study, *Spelling the Word: George Herbert and the Bible*. Her poems and translations have been set to music, notably in *Chana's Story*, a song cycle by David Del Tredici, and *The Song of Songs*, a cantata by the late Jorge Liderman.

Her honors include the Poetry Society of America's Alice Fay di Castagnola Award, the Felix Pollak Prize in Poetry, the PEN Award for Poetry in Translation (with Chana Kronfeld), the Meringoff Poetry Award, two Pushcart Prizes, two fellowships from the National Endowment for the Arts, the Writers Exchange Award of Poets & Writers, and the Discovery Award of the 92nd Street Y Poetry Center.

A native New Yorker, Bloch has lived in Berkeley since 1967. She is married to Dave Sutter and has two grown sons, Benjamin and Jonathan, from her marriage to Ariel Bloch. Audio and video clips of readings and talks may be found on her website, www.chanabloch.com.

INDEX OF TITLES

THE AUTUMN HOUSE POETRY SERIES
Michael Simms, General Editor

The Autumn House Anthology of Contemporary American Poetry, 2nd ed.	Michael Simms, ed.
To Make It Right	Corrinne Clegg Hales • 2010, selected by Claudia Emerson
The Torah Garden	Philip Terman
Lie Down with Me	Julie Suk
The Beds	Martha Rhodes
The Water Books	Judith Vollmer
Sheet Music	Robert Gibb
Natural Causes	Brian Brodeur • 2011, selected by Denise Duhamel
Miraculum	Ruth L. Schwartz
Late Rapturous	Frank X. Gaspar
Bathhouse Betty	Matt Terhune*
Irish Coffee	Jay Carson*
A Raft of Grief	Chelsea Rathburn • 2012, selected by Stephen Dunn
A Poet's Sourcebook: Writings about Poetry, from the Ancient World to the Present	Dawn Potter, ed.
Landscape with Female Figure: New and Selected Poems, 1982–2002	Andrea Hollander
Prayers of an American Wife	Victoria Kelly*
Rooms of the Living	Paul Martin*
Mass of the Forgotten	James Tolan
The Moons of August	Danusha Laméris • 2013, selected by Naomi Shihab Nye
The Welter of Me and You	Peter Schireson*
Swimming in the Rain: New and Selected Poems, 1980–2015	Chana Bloch
Sugar Run Road	Ed Ochester

• Winner of the annual Autumn House Poetry Prize
* *Coal Hill Review* chapbook series

DESIGN AND PRODUCTION

Text and cover design: Chiquita Babb

Cover painting: *fullflood #15*, oil on canvas, (c) Donna Brookman 2012. Used by permission of the artist. All rights reserved.

Donna Brookman is an artist whose work has been exhibited nationally and internationally, most recently in a solo exhibition of the *fullflood* paintings at Thomas Paul Fine Art in Los Angeles. *Fullflood #15* is the last in a series of paintings that "capture so beautifully . . . the elusive space between representation and abstraction" (Stephen Greenblatt). The series of *fullflood* paintings and the Greenblatt essay may be found on her website, www.donnabrookman.net. Brookman is a long-time resident of Berkeley, California.

Author photograph: Peg Skorpinski

This book is typeset in Monotype Dante, a mid-twentieth-century serif font created as a collaboration between typeface artist Giovanni Mardersteig and punch-cutter Charles Malin. The font's name came from its first use— a 1955 printing of Boccaccio's *Trattatello in Laude di Dante*.

Display elements are set in Gill Sans, a sans serif font designed by Eric Gill and released by Monotype for use in 1928.